*Plants for the
Winter Garden*

PLANTS

for the

WINTER GARDEN

Perennials, Grasses,
Shrubs, and Trees
to Add Interest
in the Cold and Snow

WARREN LEACH

TIMBER PRESS
PORTLAND, OREGON

Timber Press
Workman Publishing
Hachette Book Group, Inc.
1290 Avenue of the Americas
New York, New York 10104
timberpress.com

Timber Press is an imprint of Workman Publishing, a division of Hachette Book Group, Inc. The Timber Press name and logo are registered trademarks of Hachette Book Group, Inc.

Printed in China on responsibly sourced paper

Text design by Brooke Johnson Design
Cover design by Vincent James

The publisher is not responsible for websites (or their content) that are not owned by the publisher.

The Hachette Speakers Bureau provides a wide range of authors for speaking events. To find out more, go to hachettespeakersbureau.com or email hachettespeakers@hbgusa.com.

ISBN 978-1-60469-926-5

A catalog record for this book is available from the Library of Congress.

This book is dedicated to the charming woman that I met many years ago at the preview gala of the New England Spring Flower Show. Debi Hogan continues to be by my side as a loving wife and a gardening companion. My deepest affection and thanks go to Debi for her discerning editing, encouraging guidance, and endless patience.

Icy crystals of hoarfrost encrust the red fruit of staghorn sumac.

CONTENTS

The Spirit Path at the Abby Aldrich Rockefeller Garden, where a formal layout ensures the garden will retain structure even once the mosses and low native groundcovers are blanketed with snow.

Preface

I grew up on a farm in rural Holden, Maine. My passion for gardening developed early, starting at the age of five. My first flower garden was a border of summer-blooming annuals started from seed and planted in front of existing herbaceous perennial peonies, delphiniums, and daylilies. A fragrant lilac anchored the back of the border. I learned the skills of gardening at the nurturing hands of my mother. She instilled in me a love for both cultivated and wild landscapes and a discerning eye for seeing subtle beauty.

Our hilltop property was diverse in its environmental character. I roamed and explored it all, from hayfields bounded by rough laid stone walls to unmown pastures painted with wildflowers. The farm's hundreds of acres of terrain also varied greatly. There were rolling fields and steep hillsides bolstered by granite ledges that descended to tussocked swamps and woodland streams. Its tree species were characteristic of both eastern hardwood forest and boreal coniferous growth. The woods were densely forested with birch, beech, maple, and oak, as well as evergreen spruce, pine, and fir.

The view from the upper field revealed a panorama of hills and a glimmer of water from Blue Hill Bay in the distance. At the convergence of Blue Hill Bay and Frenchman Bay are Mount Desert Island and Acadia National Park. The island scenery with its majestic topography of mountains that meet the sea, in conjunction with several superlative gardens, was an essential locus of my formative horticultural education. I count myself fortunate to have first experienced the Abby Aldrich Rockefeller Garden in Seal Harbor, and Thuya Garden and the Asticou Azalea Garden in Northeast Harbor, as a young adolescent.

The Abby Aldrich Rockefeller Garden represents Beatrix Farrand's genius. The garden is masterful for its harmony of contrasts. Woods of dark spruce carpeted in moss is the setting of this garden, enclosed by high, pink stucco walls topped with ochre-glazed tiles from China. The garden entrance is aligned on a long axis that forms the Spirit Path. Its progression is flanked by a series of stone Korean tomb figures and ends with a stele that creates a focal point. The Spirit Path's formal regimentation is in direct contrast to its irregular planting design of green moss combined with native groundcovers: bunchberry (*Cornus canadensis*), wintergreen (*Gaultheria procumbens*), and lowbush blueberry (*Vaccinium angustifolium*). The garden's strong geometric patterning is a dynamic foil to its luxuriant and floriferous planting. This same strong structural patterning is also key to designing a winter garden.

Allowing the white sands of the zen garden in the Asticou Azalea Garden to stand in for snow is a helpful way to think about how a garden's structure might look in winter.

The genesis of Thuya Garden and the Asticou Azalea Garden in Northeast Harbor is a heroic response to Beatrix Farrand's decision to dismantle her Reef Point Gardens in Bar Harbor in 1956. Through the design talent of Charles Savage and the philanthropic generosity of John D. Rockefeller, Jr., two extraordinary gardens arose using plant specimens transplanted from Farrand's collection. The two gardens, though in close proximity in the same coastal Maine village, reflect themes that are a world apart. Whereas Thuya's plan is based on axial, English-style herbaceous borders, Asticou's design emulates a Japanese stroll garden featuring Farrand's Ericaceae collection. Savage imbued the stroll garden with appropriate Japanese accoutrements, including artful rock placements, stone snow lanterns, and a Ryoan-ji-inspired sand garden. Both of these gardens are magical places. I've been visiting them for half a century, and they are still a favorite destination.

Across Frenchman Bay from Bar Harbor is the Schoodic Peninsula, a mainland parcel of Acadia National Park. Schoodic's beauty is different from

Mount Desert. If the mountainous island is characterized by its verticality, Schoodic is all about the horizontal. Schoodic Point is a monolithic geologic formation. Expansive granite ledges step down in a series of shelves to the open, roiling Atlantic Ocean. The granite ledges are seamed with fissures and chasms. Basalt dikes form contrasting black bands of igneous rock that has been polished smooth by eons of ocean waves. Belying its tumultuous origin, Schoodic today is a peaceful and serene setting. The view to the horizon becomes indistinct from the foreground of blue sea. The landscape is accentuated by the horizontal silhouettes of jack pines (*Pinus banksiana*). Sections of Schoodic's landscape are, in fact, like an abstraction of a Japanese garden. The jack pines and black spruce (*Picea mariana*) appear like bonsai, though their stunted forms are sculpted not by secateurs, but by the wind. Their stature is dwarfed by the cultural environment, growing out of fissures in granite. Shallow pools of water are formed in the granite outcropping, adding diversity to the gardenesque planting. The pools offer a home to hummocks of sedges, slender blue flag (*Iris prismatica*), and cranberries (*Vaccinium macrocarpon*). Lowbush blueberry (*Vaccinium angustifolium*) and mountain cranberry (*Vaccinium vitis-idaea* ssp. *minus*) form low thickets and outline a circuit of solid granite paths. The fine, heath-like foliage of crowberry (*Empetrum nigrum*) imparts a distinctive sweet scent to the surroundings.

Schoodic's wild beauty may be serene and contemplative, but horticulturally it is a harsh environment. However, many of the native plants growing there can be highlights in residential winter gardens.

Preparing for winter on our rural Maine farm was more about survival than pursuing aesthetics. We planted enough crops to consume throughout summer and to store to last the long winter. To sustain our family, my mother prepared and canned hundreds of jars of green beans, beets, tomatoes, relishes, jams, and jellies. In fall we harvested potatoes, turnips, carrots, squash, and apples and stored them in bins in the earthen-floored cellar of our eighteenth-century farmhouse. Readying for winter also entailed banking the house with evergreen boughs, an archaic custom practiced in rural northern New England. My brothers and I cut long branches of spruce, fir, and white pine and laboriously dragged them from the woods across acres of hayfields to the house. We interwove the boughs against the house's granite foundation, forming a dense framework to hold insulating snow. The wreath of evergreen boughs nestled against the white-painted clapboards is a fond winter memory of my childhood.

The town's public works department prepared for winter by putting up hundreds of feet of wood-slatted snow fencing across our open fields. It caught the blowing snow in its lee, creating mounding drifts that kept the road from becoming deeply buried. The linear snow fence acted as an abstract sculpture on the winter landscape. I remember one winter when the snow drifted to the height of the eaves of the house. We dug a tunnel through it to get to the barn to feed the chickens! I've earned my winter snow cred.

For the last forty years, I've called Massachusetts home. Gardening continues to be an avocation as well as a vocation. My gardening education was forged in my early youth, tempered with formal horticultural instruction at the University of Maine, and has been honed through years of practice. I have worked in many aspects of ornamental horticulture, as a nurseryman growing plants and as a landscape horti-culturist; designing, building, and planting distinctive landscapes. I relish sharing my knowledge and passion of horticulture and design by lecturing and teaching and through Tranquil Lake Nursery, purveying exceptional plants and creating distinctive designs.

During my lifetime of gardening in New England, the rhythm of the changing seasons has become ingrained into my consciousness. This pattern of transitions from spring to summer marching into autumn and winter has become a familiar milieu. I've come to realize that, contrary to the conventional adage attributed to long acquaintances, for me familiarity breeds esteem and arouses amazement. This wonderment is amplified in response to scenes that may appear to be out of place and a surprise, such as flowers that bloom outside your window in the dead of winter. How incredible is that! The winter season offers a host of opportunities to express gardening creativity.

In compiling this book, I've photographed favorite winter landscapes and plants from Washington, D.C. to Pennsylvania, New York, Connecticut, Rhode Island, Massachusetts, and Maine. In Massachusetts, I design gardens with plants suitable for Zone 5, and with microclimates ranging to Zone 6 and 7. Many of the plants I have listed here are hardy to Zone 4.

I am reminded of some philosophical insights Sir George Sitwell distills in his 1910 opus *On the Making of Gardens*: "the power of novelty sharpens sensations... Surprise may add to novelty the shock of contradiction, and if care has been taken to make the expectation less than reality, we shall have added the thrill of wonder. Indeed, in every great garden there should be some element of wonder or surprise, if only to make recollection more vivid."

I hope this book conveys a contagious warmth and passion for planting winter landscapes. Release your inner child to the thrill of wonderment at viewing a garden covered with freshly fallen snow, the crystalline incrustations of hoarfrost, ghostly elongated shadows, and especially the flowers of witch hazels blooming against the mottled bark of *Stewartia*.

—*Warren P. Leach*

The Schoodic Peninsula's horticultural diversity is an inspiration. The unforgiving landscape allows us to draw parallels to the possibilities of the surprising conditions plants can tolerate in winter landscapes.

A dramatic sugar maple shadow acts as abstract art on a field of snow.

Introduction

The seasons of spring, summer, and autumn tend to benignly meld into one another, though each season has its distinct bloom sequence and growth cycles. Winter, by contrast, is a season whose beginning is marked by the abrupt drama of the end of plant growth.

Though active plant growth pauses, the winter garden is still very much alive.

The winter season in the garden offers exquisite nuances and stark contrasts. It is the season of long shadows. In winter, the low angle of the sun bestows a quality of light that artists and photographers seek, and sunlight should be considered a design element of the winter garden in its own right. Ornamental traceries transform and embellish the garden. Rays of sun appear to gild the pendant seedheads of Japanese clethra (*Clethra barbinervis*), turning them into golden lavalieres, and illuminate fuzzy magnolia buds.

Winter is abundant in metaphysical imagery that seems to be contradictory. Although the winter garden may appear austere and stark, it is actually quite rich in structure, style, pattern, and form. The lively and vibrant essence that animates the winter garden comes from a bounty of verdant foliage found in conifers and broadleaf evergreen trees, shrubs, and herbaceous perennials. This exuberance can also be fortified by vividly pigmented twigs, ornamental bark, and brightly colored fruits displayed on trees and shrubs. There are even some flowers that flourish in the winter garden, contributing a colorful array of blooms that unfurl in defiance of the whims of winter weather.

In New England and other locales in northern latitudes, winter snow cover is often ephemeral, unreliable, and not necessarily a constant seasonal condition. Artists and savvy gardeners know that instead of contempt, we should be thankful for snow when it comes, admire its transcendent beauty, and contemplate its properties. A winter snow brings metamorphosis to the garden. A fresh, new snow is familiar yet novel—almost magical. It creates a surreal landscape with a dream-like quality. A layer of white snow is a blank canvas for displays of inky shadows. It transmutes the landscape into a gallery full of back-lit silhouettes. Snow appears colorless and white because it absorbs a broad spectrum of red light while reflecting blue tints. In the garden, a blanket of snow transforms all into a monochromatic, minimalist landscape. The enigmatic nature of snow radically changes the landscape to an impressionistic state.

In the bright, clear winter sunlight, the seed heads of *Clethra barbinervis* (right) appear gilded, and the fuzzy buds of *Magnolia stellata* (bottom) are lit as if from within.

Another paradoxical characteristic of snow is its ability to simultaneously obscure and reveal. Three-dimensional design features are accentuated above a concealing layer of white snow. The snow magnifies the sculptural forms of trees, walls, fences, and arbors in the garden as they rise above blanketing drifts. Snow elevates even mundane structures into artistic works. A white veil of snow fused to the surface of stone walls transforms a loosely laid feature into a refined sculpture: a monochromatic composition of light and shadow.

A zen garden in the Japanese karesansui style has many elements that are similar to a snowy landscape. This type of garden is a surrealist landscape in which white sand is raked into patterns that represent rippled waves in the vastness of the sea meeting islands of judiciously placed stones. The Asticou Azalea Garden in Maine is an excellent example, captivating and inspiring to view. The winter garden offers as much wondrous opportunity for contemplation and reflection as a zen garden, especially viewed through a window from the comfort and warmth inside the house.

Though winter's demeanor is defined by sub-freezing temperatures, the season is certainly not static. Winter's temperament is one of flux; temperatures shift radically from November to March, from polar plunges to midwinter thaws. Precipitation runs the gamut of water's physical properties, from liquid rain to frozen icy crystals falling as pelts of sleet or puffed up into downy drifts of snow. The spiny spangled crystals of hoarfrost encrusting twigs are perhaps the most wondrous winter garden phenomenon. Hoarfrost is exceptionally ephemeral, only lasting an hour or so after sunrise. Its spectacle is an impetus for early morning garden walks.

Ice and snow covering the branches of trees present clashing qualities that may result with divergent outcomes. Sparkling and glistening like diamonds,

Hamamelis virginiana 'Wicked' has no scruples about blooming despite snow.

Snow can transform a tussocky meadow into a white-capped seascape evocative of a Winslow Homer canvas.

branches and twigs encased in a thick rime of ice may well be a pinnacle of rare beauty. Laden and bejeweled to a few degrees over the tipping point, however, this smashing spectacle becomes a cascading disaster.

Weather is not the only dynamic element to contemplate in designing a winter garden. Cold temperatures bring on metamorphic changes in many plants, intensifying color pigmentation in woody stems and augmenting foliage coloration, which heightens their winter ornamentation. The bark of *Acer palmatum* 'Sango-kaku' and *Cornus alba* 'Westonbirt' become vivid red with winter's onset. The stems of *Acer negundo* 'Winter Lightning' and *Cornus sericea* 'Flaviramea' turn egg-yolk yellow. Cold transforms the green mantle of *Pinus virginiana* 'Wate's Golden' to an electrifying chrome yellow. The winter complection of *Rhododendron* 'PJM' shifts from olive-green to the color of polished cordovan leather. *Sasa veitchii* sports green leaves until a cold snap sparks a variegated transformation, icing the leaf margins to white.

In Massachusetts, winter lasts five months! This is not hyperbole. Winter's formal arrival deviates considerably, depending upon the date to which you adhere. The rival denominators are meteorological

Even simple garden structures exude presence and solemnity against the pure white canvas of snow.

winter, which begins with December, and astronomical winter, which arrives twenty days later, the traditional date of the winter solstice and the shortest day of the year. I define the start of winter as horticultural winter, which commences in Massachusetts in mid-November after a hard, killing frost. The winter season does not begin on a fixed date, but starts with the ending of plant growth. Horticultural winter also extends past its traditional astronomical end on March 21st and even past the first of April. In New

Winter gardens filled with snow and Japanese gardens planned around expanses of white sand offer similarly calming vistas to observers.

Fleeting hoarfrost on *Poncirus* (left), *Asclepias syriaca* (center), and *Aronia arbutifolia* (right) makes a chance encounter with it on an early winter morning feel like a true gift.

England, snow is not uncommon on April Fools' Day, and killing frosts are a reality into May. Taking into account this delineating methodology, winter does indeed last for five months.

This reality is by no means cause for a gardener's depression: It is cause for an enthusiastic embrace of the winter garden season. After all, it is a substantial portion of the garden calendar.

Making an engaging winter garden entails some of the same design processes as those involved in fashioning other seasonal gardens. Categorizing site conditions and preparing plant lists detailing ornamental values and cultural requirements is an important beginning. Winter plant highlights include colorful bark and fruit; evergreen foliage attributes of trees, shrubs, and herbaceous perennials; and

especially wintertime blooms. Regardless of the season, some aspects of the garden like colorful fruits and flowers will always be ephemeral. The red fruit of winterberry holly is often gobbled up by robins and other birds, sometimes not lasting through December, while some winter-flowering witch hazels may last for many weeks, and the bracts of hellebores can persist for months, outperforming summer-blooming perennials.

To be most successful in designing a winter garden, heed the hard-and-fast rule of implementing structure, which is to say including enduring forms that will stand up against winter's vagaries of snow and ice. This essential structure can include both arrangements of plants and built objects, such as walls, trellises, tuteurs, and pergolas. Clipped hedges can stand in

Acer palmatum 'Sango-kaku' features intensely red stems that stand out in winter.

Both *Pinus virginiana* 'Wate's Golden' (top) and *Rhododendron* 'PJM' (bottom) go through intense color shifts in cold weather.

for walls and architectural forms. Include trees with distinctive shapes such as fastigiate or weeping—they will stand out against the horizon and also cast intriguing shadows on a wintry landscape blurred by a white mantle.

Deciduous trees have shed their vivid leaves to show off their sculptural silhouettes. Their beauty is freely expressed in their colorful bark-clothed boles. Winter is the season of *Stewartia pseudocamellia*, *Acer griseum*, and *Betula papyrifera*. The ornamental, exfoliating bark of Chinese filbert (*Corylus fargesii*) and Heritage river birch (*Betula nigra* 'Cully') glows luminously when backlit by the low angle of the winter sun. Such trees with beautiful bark, planted either as single specimens or in groves, add a unique quality to the winter landscape.

Deep drifts of snow obliterate subtle garden design features. Design plantings and structural elements to rise above the snow line. Be adventurous in the winter garden—plant a grove of fastigiate weeping conifers, such as *Picea glauca* 'Pendula', which shed snow, resist ice breakage, and cast alluring shadows.

The design principle of occult balance, contrasting diversity with repetition, holds true in the winter garden. Evergreen borders and coniferous hedges certainly have winter presence, but if they dominate, the landscape may create a somber impression. Mix your winter plant palette with the glossy foliage of broadleaf evergreens as a foil for colorful bark, fruit, and flowers.

Stewartia pseudocamellia (left) and *Corylus fargesii* (right) have barks with inherently interesting texture.

Off-season attention to new plant placement means plantings of *Betula nigra* 'Cully' (top left) and *Hamamelis ×intermedia* 'Diane', *Acer negundo* 'Winter Lightning' (above), or *Malus* 'Louisa' (bottom left) against evergreens can provide striking moments of color contrast and deeply satisfying texture combinations.

PART I
LASTING FORMS AND COLORS

Chapter One

Enduring
Remnants

The remnants of many summer-flowering perennials are attractive in the winter garden. Savvy gardeners are selective during fall garden cleanup and cut back only those herbaceous perennials without winter substance. Thoughtful removal of some spent foliage that may harbor pest or fungal diseases is an appropriate garden practice. However, there are rationales for leaving the stubble of perennials and remnants of flowers in place. Many of these spent flower heads contain seeds that are valuable food for birds in the lean fall and winter seasons.

In late winter, Olympian mullein stands as stately as it was in full summer bloom; new growth forms rosettes that remain evergreen throughout the coldest months.

Remnant foliage stems and leaves also provide invaluable shelter and nesting sites for overwintering beneficial insects and pollinators. Species of native solitary bees and wasps create small nests just beneath the soil or in dead plant stems. Various members of the order Lepidoptera, which includes butterflies and moths, overwinter in all life cycle stages, from egg to caterpillar, chrysalis, and adult. Cold hardy and colorful woolly bear caterpillars hibernate under the protection of fallen leaves.

Some plant remnants still have the stamina to impart a substantial presence in the winter garden. Remaining skeletal fragments of flowers may deteriorate from their former glory but retain their structure. The six-foot-tall candelabrum of *Verbascum olympicum*, for example, is a garden favorite of mine in summer and winter. Its branched, towering torches are especially beautiful when flocked with white snow. *Verbascum olympicum* is a biennial species that also reliably self-seeds in the garden so long as its flower stalks are not prematurely cut down. Its new growth forms large rosettes of felted foliage that remain evergreen throughout winter.

Culver's root (*Veronicastrum virginicum*), though not as large as mullein, is a herbaceous perennial with woody flower stems that support candelabra spikes. Even the simple and flat, umbel flowers of showy stonecrop (*Hylotelephium spectabile*), which were once colorful pink landing pads for butterflies in the summer, are still attractive as brown flat disks that collect winter snow.

The former lawn at this small suburban property was eliminated in the front area between the house and the street. It was replaced by a mixture of herbaceous perennials and shrubs that bloom from spring to fall frost. A salt-tolerant and snowplow-resistant border of two shrubs, northern bayberry (*Morella pensylvanica*) and sweet fern (*Comptonia peregrina*), now separates the street from the sunny front garden. The perennial planting was designed to cover the ground and act as a living mulch. The herbaceous plants' spreading foliage and clumping crowns protect the soil from extremes of heat and cold. They also act to suppress weeds and prevent erosion in this small garden. It was essential to select perennials with attractive leaves as well as

TOP *Veronicastrum virginicum* seedheads in frost.

RIGHT *Hylotelephium spectabile*

Summer and winter views of a mixed herbaceous garden designed specifically to be drought tolerant and to sustain structural interest and winter beauty

flowers to grow and mix together without rivalry, and thrive as a unified matrix. Wine-leaf cinquefoil (*Sibbaldiopsis tridentata*) happily mingles around the crowns of sunny perennials and was a key plant in establishing a green mulch here.

A bluestone walkway connects to an elliptical entry landing. It divides and structures the garden spaces. The tiny, evergreen leaves of creeping thyme (*Thymus serpyllum*) and persistent, silver foliage of beach wormwood (*Artemisia stelleriana* 'Silver Brocade') cover the ground. They knit together the clump-forming crowns of Russian sage (*Perovskia atriplicifolia*) and Arkansas bluestar (*Amsonia hubrichtii*). Russian sage displays majestic violet-blue flowers on pyramidally branched sprays in August, after which their woody stems are coated in silver-white, and finally they take on a luminous presence in the garden. To replicate this look, leave the stems to embellish the winter garden, then prune them back to a height of eight to twelve inches at axillary buds in the spring.

'Golden Fleece' goldenrod (*Solidago sphacelata* 'Golden Fleece') and 'Herrenhausen' oregano (*Origanum laevigatum* 'Herrenhausen') edge the stone walkway with their bright yellow and mauve summer blooms. They maintain a winter presence with the remnant fragments of condensed flower spikes. Shrubby 'Berggarten' sage (*Salvia officinalis* 'Berggarten') maintains its silver-gray foliage all winter. It is planted with Russian sage along the base of the house. The gray-green foliage of yarrow (*Achillea* ×'Moonshine') also persists in the winter, as do the remnants of its flat yellow flower umbels. Letterman's ironweed (*Vernonia lettermannii* 'Iron Butterfly') stands in defiance of winter with remnant flowers and fine foliage that are still very recognizable. Mixed with

the beige, gray, and brown of the garden's winter duff are the bright evergreen leaves of candytuft (*Iberis sempervirens* 'Purity'). There are also shrubs: the dark green foliage of 'Nova Scotia' dwarf inkberry holly (*Ilex glabra* 'Nova Scotia') and *Daphne* ×*transatlantica* 'Eternal Fragrance' combined with the red fruit of winterberry holly (*Ilex verticillata* 'Winter Red') add to the matrix of herbaceous perennials.

This garden is environmentally well designed and thrives with little supplemental care. The nubbly fabric of the remnant, ornamental stubble stands throughout the winter, providing ecological habitat as well as wintry beauty.

Grasses also make appearances in this garden, and several species earn their place in winter gardens. Broom bluestem (*Andropogon virginicus*) and little bluestem (*Schizachyrium scoparium*) are native grasses that stand erect in winter, unbowed by snow. They were once classified together in the genus *Andropogon*. Both are found growing throughout a wide swathe of the United States, from Maine west to Idaho and south to Florida and Arizona. They are both clump-forming, green-foliaged grasses that require full sun and well-drained soil conditions.

Little bluestem is one of the dominant grasses found in the central prairies. Its new taxonomical identity also marks ornamental distinctions that are revealed in the cultivated landscape. *Schizachyrium scoparium* 'Standing Ovation' is one of many little bluestem cultivars selected for their striking glaucous-blue colored foliage in summer. It grows two to three feet tall in upright clumps. In the fall, the blades of 'Standing Ovation' are highlighted with streaks of maroon and burgundy, eventually turning to amber. The foliage of some blue-leafed cultivars of

Solidago sp.

Salvia officinalis

Ilex glabra

Ilex verticillata

Andropogon virginicus

Schizachyrium scoparium

Pennisetum alopecuroides

Hakonechloa macra

Sporobolus heterolepis

Schizachyrium scoparium is inclined to "lodge," or flop, even when grown in dry conditions.

In contrast, broom bluestem (*Andropogon virginicus*) always holds its green foliage rigidly upright. Unfortunately for gardeners, there are no glaucous blue-leafed forms of this plant. If the main focus of a landscape planting of these grasses is to achieve sustained beauty for the five-month-long winter season that extends from November through March, broom bluestem is the best choice of the two genera. A sizable swathe of its copper- and amber-colored linear leaves

provides a knockout display throughout winter. I cut down my small, five-thousand-square-foot meadow of broom bluestem in early April.

Self-seeding is an important factor to consider when choosing grasses for a mixed herbaceous border as opposed to a meadow. Both *Schizachyrium* and *Andropogon* freely self seed, and without attention, they can become weedy in a small garden. Though not as tall as little bluestem, blue oat grass (*Helictotrichon sempervirens* 'Sapphire') is a much better behaved, non-seeding, and beautiful blue-foliaged grass for the mixed perennial garden.

Dwarf fountain grass (*Pennisetum alopecuroides* 'Hameln') and Japanese woodland grass (*Hakonechloa macra*) are clump-forming Asian grasses that reach about two feet tall with remnant foliage that has an ornamental winter presence. Their cultural requirements and decorative forms are very different. 'Hameln' dwarf fountain grass forms a tussock of narrow green leaves that turn golden in the fall. It's characterized by its arched leaves and stems terminated by feathery bottlebrush flowers. The remnant bristled seedheads drift above straw-yellow leaves and glow in the winter sun. This plant thrives in full sun and dry soil conditions.

Japanese woodland grass (*Hakonechloa macra*) grows best in partial shade and moisture-retentive soils. It is a very elegant grass, with arching, linear green leaves that widen in the middle and taper at either end, giving it a graceful appearance. The flowers are formed from terminal arched panicles. The remnant foliage and seedheads take on a light bronze winter coloring.

Some large ornamental grasses present more maintenance chores for the gardener than their winter ornamentation provides. Often, by late winter, they appear disheveled and have lost their charm. The coarse stalks and leaves of many *Miscanthus sinensis* cultivars do not readily disintegrate, which makes the task of cutting them back onerous. One very tall grass species has practical horticultural value, however. *Miscanthus floridulus* produces eight-foot-tall bamboo-like stems. They are so rigidly sturdy that I cut them down in November and store them in bundles to use as garden stakes the following year.

A final grass to consider is prairie dropseed (*Sporobolus heterolepis*), a drought-tolerant species that grows into mounded hummocks. Its narrow, green leaf blades flow to form an undulating, tousled pile of foliage. Its winter shape is a golden tan mophead. Green growth emerges from its pate in spring.

Chapter Two

Evergreen Broadleaf and Coniferous Trees and Shrubs

reen, the color of chlorophyll, is the color of life. A verdant garden appears fresh and alive. Green foliage also warms up an otherwise bleak winter landscape, reassuring us through dark months that life persists even in the most severe conditions. Broadleaf and coniferous evergreen trees and shrubs are essential to designing and planting a luxuriant and welcoming winter landscape.

Many plants that hold their leaves through the frozen winter have leaf adaptations that help them defy drought and water loss. Happily, these functional characteristics sometimes result in structures gardeners consider highly ornamental. The foliage of some conifers has evolved into narrow, needle-like leaves that, first and foremost, assist in reducing evaporation during both frozen winters and dry summers. The silver-colored, glaucous, waxy coating on the cuticle of many needled conifers also helps the tree survive by forming a water-resistant barrier and reflecting the heat of the sun. Many magnolias have thick, lustrous leaves that act to slow transpiration and conserve water. In the wild, you can often find these types of plants growing in the same areas. Tough broadleaf evergreen hollies, such as *Ilex opaca*, and pitch pine *(Pinus rigida)* cling tenaciously to edges of Cape Cod coastal dunes, while dwarf forms of *Ilex glabra* and jack pine (*Pinus banksiana*) cover rocky ledges in Halifax, Nova Scotia. We can take cues from nature and combine these at home to bring green beauty to the winter garden.

Evergreen foliage also provides an attractive background that acts as a neutral color backdrop for the array of colors found in winter flowers, fruits, and other ornamental features. Green is well known as the complementary color to red, and it intensifies all the hues falling within that basic description, from coral pink to crimson. It also accents the scarlet-red fruits of winterberry holly.

"Evergreen" is the word used for plants that retain their foliage through the winter, but this is an oversimplification. Foliage exhibits many diverse and complex attributes of color, texture, and form. The list of gradations of the color green would be nearly as long as the

Evergreens can add important and varied texture and interest to the winter garden.

list of evergreen trees and shrubs that may be used successfully in winter garden design. The color spectrum for foliage ranges from yellow green to blue green and reddish bronze. *The Royal Horticultural Society Colour Chart*, the horticultural industry's standard guide for identifying the colors of biological samples, codes several hundred gradations of hue, value, and chroma of "green." The foliage characteristics of plants, of course, don't simply conform to a particular color chip—their representational expression is more complex than color alone. Sunlight and oblique shadows constantly change how we perceive a combined mixture of hue, texture, and foliar form.

A critical examination of the color and substance of evergreen plants is a study in the absorption and reflection of white light. Leaf surfaces, in their diversity—coarse or fine, rough or smooth, matte or glossy, broad or linear—are all foliar values that interact with light differently. For example, the standard for glossiness, or the specular reflection of a surface, is based on the properties of highly polished black glass. Manufactured surface coatings such as automotive paint or varnish are comparatively measured in gloss units by a gloss meter instrument. This representational calculation can be symbolically extrapolated to the qualities of a leaf surface. The fine linear needles of conifers such as pine and spruce primarily absorb light. In general, conifers would rate low on a gloss scale, and therefore, they appear as dark forms in the landscape.

Foliar adaptations allow different plants to thrive in harsh conditions. Narrow needles, such as those of *Pinus banksiana* (top), are a modification to reduce evaporation. Magnolias such as *Magnolia virginiana* 'Henry Hicks' (middle) and hollies like *Ilex opaca* (bottom) have evolved thick, waxy leaves that conserve water.

Coniferous evergreen foliage sets off the colorful features of other winter garden stars, like the cinnamon-red exfoliating bark of *Acer griseum*.

Over thirty years ago, I had an enlightening and memorable experience regarding this quality of light reflection in leaves. It occurred while I was collaborating with a theatrical lighting technician to design a night lighting scheme for a garden. The garden was bordered by mature native white pines (*Pinus strobus*), and their fine-needled foliage absorbed the light so completely that it caused the coniferous background of the garden to remain dark. It was barely lit regardless of the thousands of lumina projected.

CONIFERS

Many of our native wooded landscapes in areas that have extended winters are forested with a dark coniferous background, so a number of native coniferous evergreens are familiar to many gardeners. The pointed spires of balsam fir and white spruce, for example, produce the dark, thick evergreen stands that outline Maine's rocky coast. Throughout the northeast, these are accompanied by Canadian hemlock (*Tsuga canadensis*) and several species of pine, ranging from the towering masts of "king's pine" or eastern white pine (*Pinus strobus*) to the contorted forms of pitch pine (*Pinus rigida*) and jack pine (*Pinus banksiana*). Cedars such as *Chamaecyparis thyoides* and *Thuja occidentalis* ring the edges of wooded swamps. Red cedar (*Juniperus virginiana* and *Juniperus communis*) encroaches on upland meadows.

CYPRESS AND CEDAR
Calocedrus, *Chamaecyparis*, *Thujopsis*, and *Thuja* are genera of conifers with leaves composed of overlapped scales intricately braided into flattened, frond-like sprays. Though individual samples of their foliage may appear very similar, their overall visual aspects differ significantly, especially in their color tones of green. The geometric configuration of their foliage reveals their identity, as the specific planar arrangement of their flattened foliage can be recognized from a distance. Their various highlights and shadows tell us whether their leaf orientation is held vertically or horizontally. Light reveals this intrinsic nature and clearly shows the textural difference between *Chamaecyparis obtusa* and *Thuja plicata*, for example. These textural profiles, coupled with an individual conifer's cultural requirements, play an important design role in planting selection and combinations.

The blue-green foliage of China fir (*Cunninghamia lanceolata* 'Glauca')—a member of the cypress family, despite its common name—covers whorled branches with linear, needle-shaped twisted leaves that are set in a double-ranked spiral arrangement. Its glaucous foliage appears featherlike. A dark, glossy leafed background of Blue Princess holly (Ilex ×meserveae Blue Princess) or *Berberis julianae* accents a shift in color and texture that complements China fir.

UMBRELLA PINE
Japanese umbrella pine (*Sciadopitys verticillata*) takes exception to the generalization that conifer needles are dark and dull. Its whorls of needles are glossy green and highly reflective, gleaming in winter sun. The spoke-like arrangement of thick needles is a singular and distinguishing feature of this tree. It is not a true pine, but a unique genus containing only one species within its own family, the Sciadopityaceae. This single extant species grows in the mountains of the Japanese islands of Honshu, Shikoku, and Kyushu. Like ginkgo,

Though Hinoki cypress (*Chamaecyparis obtusa*, left) and western red cedar (*Thuja plicata*, right) have foliage composed of scaly fronds, their habit and orientation are quite different, meaning they reflect light in opposite ways in the garden.

Spiral leaves of *Cunninghamia lanceolata* 'Glauca' show well against a backdrop of shiny holly.

it has no living relatives; however, horticulturists have selected and propagated many varying ornamental forms of the sole species. Dr. Sidney Waxman, Professor Emeritus at the University of Connecticut, was noted for his contributions to propagating and introducing many distinguished selections of conifers, including umbrella pine. He was known for shooting down propagules from witches' brooms—a branch mutation that forms congested, deformed growth—high in the treetops. His cultivar of *Sciadopitys* named 'Wintergreen', introduced in 1985, is a standard bearer with verdant foliage that doesn't bronze in winter.

Sciadopitys verticillata 'Wintergreen' features highly reflective needles, even when not obscured by ice.

BROADLEAF EVERGREENS

Some of the most stunning planting compositions of winter foliage blend the gleaming, light-reflecting attributes of broadleaf evergreens with the muted aspect of needled conifers to create a depth of contrast. For good reason, holly species and cultivars figure prominently in the winter garden, and therefore in this text—but contrary to popular belief, hollies are but one group of worthy broadleaf evergreens that shine in winter.

HOLLY AND MAHONIA

If the substantive effect of needled evergreen conifers is the absorption of light, then the polished leaves of hollies are the converse, mirroring light back brilliantly. English holly (*Ilex aquifolium*) sets the standard for the most lacquered and lustrous evergreen foliage. It is native to western and southern Europe, north Africa, and west Asia, cultivated in gardens since ancient times, and can grow into a substantial tree. Its vaunted boughs of spiny-margined foliage adorned with red fruit are a Christmastime decorating staple. English holly's northern range of hardiness is Zones 7 and 6, with added protection from desiccating winter wind. On Cape Cod and the southern coast of Massachusetts it grows best in sheltered microclimates. Hollies are dioecious, with pistillate female and pollen-bearing male flowers developing on separate plants. It also blooms and fruits on branches of the previous season's growth.

The silver hedgehog holly (*Ilex aquifolium* 'Ferox Argentea') is a male clone with spiny leaves bordered with cream-white margins. Also variegated are fruiting female cultivars 'Argentea Marginata' and 'Gold Coast',

Ilex aquifolium, the glossiest evergreen of all

Ilex aquifolium 'Gold Coast' showing evidence of leaf burn from overexposure to direct sunlight.

which benefit from protection from winter sun, which can burn their leaf margins.

The American holly (*Ilex opaca*) is a broadleaf evergreen pyramidal tree growing to forty feet tall. It produces flowers upon the current season's growth, followed by showy clusters of colorful red berries near the ends of branches. In its northern native range, it is found on Cape Cod; in south coastal Massachusetts, American holly is found growing as part of a mixed hardwood understory, often associated with red maple (*Acer rubrum*). *Ilex opaca* is hardy to Zone 5. Anecdotal observance over the last several decades indicates that the rise of median temperatures related to global climate change is allowing it to prosper farther north.

The spiny, margined evergreen foliage of American holly has a beautiful wintertime presence, though its leaves appear nearly matte compared to the lacquered leaves of English holly. The cultivar 'Jersey Princess' features dark green glossy foliage and is superior to the species. Rutgers University's New Jersey Agricultural Experiment Station holly breeding program, a project of renowned holly hybridizer Dr. Elwin Orton begun in the 1950s, produced many landmark achievements. These include *Ilex* × 'Red Beauty', the result of his interspecific hybrid cross of *Ilex aquifolium*, *Ilex rugosa*, and *Ilex pernyi*. 'Red Beauty' is a distinctive female cultivar that grows into a pyramidal form densely adorned with small, wavy, spine-edged leaves of glossy dark green. Bright red fruit adds to its winter impact.

TOP *Ilex opaca*, commonly called American holly

ABOVE *Ilex* ×'Red Beauty' set off by a backdrop of *Lindera angustifolia*

Ilex ×'Blue Prince' serves as a male pollinator. The dense, upright growth habit of 'Red Beauty' makes it an excellent narrow hedge, and it combines well with the copper-colored marcescent leaves of *Lindera angustifolia*.

The Meserve collection of 'blue' holly cultivars extends the hardiness of these lustrous evergreens to Zone 4. They are the progeny of an interspecific cross between very hardy *Ilex rugosa* and *Ilex aquifolium*. Blue Prince is the trade name of the male pollinator for the pistillate cultivar 'Blue Maid' and 'Blue Angel' as well as the commonly found variety with the trade name Blue Princess. Because these blue hollies tend to have a shrubby form of growth without a dominant central leader, they are ideal for hedges.

Koehne holly (*Ilex* ×*koehneana*) is a cross between *Ilex aquifolium* and *Ilex latifolia*. It is hardy to Zone 6, more than either of its parents. The leaves of Koehne holly are quite large with serrated leaf edges. 'Lassie' is a robust growing female cultivar that forms a uniform pyramidal tree twenty-five feet tall.

The longstalk holly (*Ilex pedunculosa*) has smooth-margined, elliptical evergreen leaves that more closely resemble the leaves of mountain laurel than those of its spiny cousins. This Japanese native is hardy in Zone 5 and grows to be a small, twenty-five-foot tree. Its common name, as well as its botanical species, refers to the distinctively long fruit stalks, or pedicels.

Evergreen, shrubby Japanese holly (*Ilex crenata*) adds a glint of reflected light in the winter garden. The venerable cultivar 'Convexa' forms a dense, rounded eight-foot shrub. Its shiny, convex leaves are like miniature thimbles, glistening through snow and frost even on dim winter days. The glossy green domed

Ilex pendunculosa, remarkable for its long fruit stalks

Ilex crenata 'Convexa' (top) and 'Drops of Gold' (above) both feature rounded, convex leaves.

foliage of *Ilex crenata* 'Drops of Gold' is daubed with yellow, lending it additional sparkle.

The native inkberry holly (*Ilex glabra*) has glossy, flat evergreen leaves. A fine-textured, mounding, suckering shrub that grows to six feet in height, it ranges from Nova Scotia, Canada, south along the east coast of the United States to Florida. Cultivars 'Shamrock', 'Compacta', and 'Densa' are common in the nursery trade. I find the best, truly compact cultivars of inkberry to be 'Nova Scotia' and 'Peggy's Cove'. They both originate from the wilds of the coast of Nova Scotia.

'Nova Scotia' was collected in Pleasantville, Nova Scotia in 1994 by Raymond R. Fielding, a high school biology teacher, keen botanist, and author of *Shrubs of Nova Scotia*. It is a female clone with lustrous dark green leaves, and its dense growth habit is only thirty-six inches tall after twenty years.

Ilex glabra 'Compacta'

The Arnold Arboretum introduced a similar compact cultivar collected from Nova Scotia in October of 1988 by their now retired propagator Jack Alexander. Jack recounts a trip to the province for a speaking engagement with the Atlantic Rhododendron and Horticultural Society, where his Canadian hosts took him sightseeing along the coast. Northwest of the fishing village of Peggy's Cove, Jack spotted a scraggly mass of inkberry holly growing on a barren, rocky outcrop, dwarfed by the harsh environment above the Atlantic Ocean. He collected cuttings and rooted them back at the Arnold Arboretum, and one plant retained the dwarf characteristic that proved to be a stable genetic trait. At the arboretum, the original plant of 'Peggy's Cove' is 22 years old, but just 48 inches high and wide.

Mahonia is a genus of plants with disjunct species that are extant in the Pacific Northwest of North America and in China, and their genus name is often used as a common name. These plants' glossy evergreen foliage is striking for its bold texture and radially whorled arrangement. The Oregon grape holly (*Mahonia aquifolium*) is neither grape nor holly. Its lustrous, pinnately compound leaves, with prickly leaflets, mimic the leaves of English holly. A suckering, spreading shrub, it grows three to four feet tall, and is hardy to Zone 5. Oregon grape holly blooms in early springtime

Mahonia aquifolium turns reddish bronze in winter.

with erect racemes of yellow flowers, followed by nodding clusters of blue fruits. As a student of horticulture at the University of Maine, I fell in love with *Mahonia aquifolium*—it survived winters with Zone 4 temperatures on the Orono campus, buried in feet of snow! Its glossy foliage is flushed with a reddish bronze overglaze in winter. It grows in the sun or shade and is an excellent shrub for creating evergreen plantings beneath conifers.

Chinese leatherleaf mahonia (*Mahonia bealei*) is another plant I favor for the winter garden. It is larger, with a coarser texture, and its tropical-looking foliage is splayed in sharply toothed, compound pinnate plumes. I have long planted it in Zone 5 landscapes, and it has thrived in gardens in Worcester, Massachusetts, with a cold-hardiness rating that is a zone colder than botanical texts reference. A sheltered east or northeast position protects it from the harsh exposure of late winter sun.

ANDROMEDA

The glossy foliage of Japanese andromeda (*Pieris japonica*) is an exceptionally beautiful addition from the Ericaceae family for the winter garden. Its leaves remain attractive in cold winter weather, unlike rhododendron leaves, which droop sadly and roll up. Andromeda foliage is also unpalatable to deer. Its additional ornamental attributes include colorful winter flower buds, which open to clusters of spring blooms. The new growth of many varieties is also brightly pigmented red. *Pieris japonica* 'Wada's Pink' is an impressive plant in the collection at the Polly Hill Arboretum on Martha's Vineyard, Massachusetts. Its panicles of flower buds are a deep rose pink color in winter. The Arnold Arboretum's archives note that it was collected by Mr. K. Wada on Mount Daisen in Japan.

Naming a plant after one's wife is a daring, if not bold, display of affection. *Pieris japonica* 'Dorothy

Mahonia bealei (left) features glossy, pointed, pinnate leaves. Combining it with Hinoki cypress (*Chamaecyparis obtusa* 'Gracilis', right) makes a verdant, texturally dynamic winter vignette.

Winter buds of *Pieris japonica*

Pieris ×'Brouwer's Beauty' was hybridized and introduced by Connecticut nurseryman Peter Brouwer. A cross between *Pieris japonica* and the southeastern US native *Pieris floribunda*, 'Brouwer's Beauty' matures to a dense evergreen shrub, six feet tall and four feet wide. Its green winter foliage complements its showy red flower panicle and buds.

Mountain andromeda (*Pieris floribunda*) does not thrive in nursery container plant production—it prefers to be field grown. Because of this, it has become a rarity in the nursery trade. Its upright branched panicles of white flower buds are a delight in the winter garden nonetheless.

LAUREL, LEUCOTHOE, AND VIBURNUM

Bay laurel (*Laurus nobilis*) is certainly not winter hardy in New England, and a cool greenhouse is required to sustain this aromatic Mediterranean evergreen. However, evergreen plants that share the vernacular name of "laurel" are valuable additions in the winter garden. Poet's laurel (*Danae racemosa*) is hardy in Zones 7–8 and grows in gardens as far north as Philadelphia, Pennsylvania. It is a winter garden gem at the Wister Center at the Scott Arboretum in Swarthmore. Its two-foot-tall arching stems display polished green foliage, but these leaves are actually cladodes: flattened, leaflike stems.

Other laurels for the winter garden include mountain laurel (*Kalmia latifolia*), English laurel (*Prunus laurocerasus*), and Japanese laurel (*Aucuba japonica*). They are all shade-tolerant, hardy broadleaf evergreens. In Hamden, Connecticut, Richard Jaynes, author of *The Laurel Book* and *Kalmia*, was at the forefront of breeding superior mountain laurel selections, including red-bud flower forms. Bloomfield,

Wycoff' was named for the wife of a New Jersey nurseryman in 1960. It continues to live up to the high expectations of its loving commemoration. Its lustrous green foliage takes on a maroon tinge in winter, and a forty-five-year-old specimen growing under a dogwood tree at Tranquil Lake Nursery is eight feet tall with a fourteen-foot spread. Other outstanding cultivars of this species were bred by Dr. Robert Ticknor at Oregon State University, including *Pieris japonica* 'Valley Valentine' and 'Valley Rose'.

Connecticut nurseryman Ludwig Hoffman was also a notable contributor to breeding excellent mountain laurel selections, and his compact-formed, red-budded cultivar 'Nathan Hale' is one of my favorites.

The lustrous dark green leaves of English laurel (*Prunus laurocerasus* 'Otto Luyken') form a low, mounded shrub. Its foliage is arranged vertically along the branches. Japanese laurel (*Aucuba japonica*), on the other hand, grows as a rounded shrub and is very tolerant of shade. Its large, leathery, and lustrous dark-green foliage accents the winter garden. Wave Hill in New York features several cultivars of *Aucuba*, including 'Serratifolia', 'Longifolia', 'Bicolor', and 'Variegata'. The variegated form is often referred to as "gold dust plant," and in New England its foliage practically looks tropical. It is hardy in Zone 5, given a protective microclimate sheltered from wind and winter sun. I have grown 'Variegata' for thirty years, planted close to the north side of a house in Seekonk, Massachusetts. Try combining cultivars of *Aucuba* or 'Otto Luyken' with those of *Leucothoe axillaris*, a spreading broadleaf evergreen shrub native to the southeast United States.

Leucothoe axillaris is another invaluable broadleaf evergreen shrub for the winter landscape. Its growth forms a mounded, suckering shrub three feet in height and width. Arching stems are clothed in glossy green, lance-shaped leaves arranged in an alternate zig-zag fashion. Leucothoe's verdant foliage acquires an attractive purplish cast in the winter. A member of the Ericaceae family, its native range is from coastal Virginia south to Florida and west to Mississippi, hence its common name, coast leucothoe. Belying its southern roots, *Leucothoe axillaris* is perfectly cold hardy and thrives in northern Zone 5 gardens. It will

Poet's laurel (*Danae racemosa*)

'Nathan Hale' mountain laurel (*Kalmia latifolia* 'Nathan Hale')

'Otto Luyken' English laurel (*Prunus laurocerasus* 'Otto Luyken')

Three cultivars of Japanese laurel (*Aucuba japonica*): 'Serratifolia' (above left), 'Longfolia' (top), and 'Variegata' (above right)

even endure Zone 4 winter temperatures with careful placement. In its wild state, leucothoe grows in moist woods and shaded thickets, yet it has proven quite tolerant of dry soils, as well as root competition from trees when planted beneath their canopies. A noted characteristic of leucothoe that is as important as its ornamental attributes is that it is unpalatable to deer.

The most recommended viburnum for cold climates in North America is *Viburnum* ×'Pragense', a lustrous broadleaf evergreen shrub that grows to 10 feet tall and wide. It originated from an interspecific cross made in 1955 in Prague, Czechoslovakia, is hardy to Zone 5 and

Leucothoe axillaris

more tolerant of cold than either of its parents, *Viburnum rhytidophyllum* and *Viburnum utile*. I have used it as an evergreen screen planted among American hollies in partial shade.

MAGNOLIA

Holly may glitter in the winter garden, but it is the evergreen sweetbay magnolia (*Magnolia virginiana* var. *australis*) that I consider the most impressive broadleaf evergreen tree to grace the snowy winter landscape. In fact, the northernmost indigenous population of *Magnolia virginiana* hails from the north shore of Massachusetts in the Cape Ann town of Magnolia. The species' native range is extensive, south to Florida, and a small disjunct group has even been found in Cuba. Though the local Massachusetts genotype is a small deciduous tree, there is a selection of the southern regional form with evergreen foliage, and it has been differentiated as a separate botanical group, now known as variety *australis*. It retains its broadleaf foliage throughout winter, even in cold southern New England, and is hardy to Zone 5.

The cultivar *Magnolia virginiana* var. *australis* 'Henry Hicks' is an excellent evergreen small tree.

Magnolia virginiana var. *australis* is well suited for climates to Zone 5.

Magnolia virginiana var. *australis* `Milton`

Magnolia virginiana var. *australis* `Green Shadow`

It was selected and registered in 1967 by the Scott Arboretum in Swarthmore, Pennsylvania. 'Henry Hicks' is named in honor of the Long Island, New York nurseryman who donated seedling magnolia plants to the arboretum in 1934. This cultivar is an upright-growing small tree, with foliage that is glossy green on top and markedly silver-white beneath. The angled arrangement of its leaves shows off this distinctively beautiful two-tone effect. I have combined this magnolia's evergreen foliage with that of American holly, 'Vardar Valley' boxwood, and fastigiate white

pine as a welcome winter greeting in a garden along an entrance drive.

Magnolia virginiana var. *australis* 'Milton' is a beautiful evergreen form that was discovered by Peter Del Tredici of the Arnold Arboretum in Boston, and several magnificent specimens are planted opposite the entrance to the Hunnewell Visitor Center there. More recently, several other evergreen forms of *australis* have been named and patented: 'Green Mile', Green Shadow', and 'Jim Wilson', which is known under the trade name Moonglow.

Magnolia virginiana 'Henry Hicks'

My experience finds *Magnolia virginiana* var. *australis* to be much more drought tolerant than most literature describes. The waxy cuticle covering its foliage suggests a biological clue to its tolerance of dry conditions, and it prospers even in an unirrigated landscape. The evergreen forms of sweetbay magnolia bloom in late June into July with highly fragrant white flowers.

More so than those of sweetbay, the bold evergreen leaves of southern magnolia (*Magnolia grandiflora*) seem like an anomaly in the New England landscape.

This tree is native to the North American coastal plain from North Carolina to Florida and eastern Texas; however, winter-tolerant cultivars such as 'Bracken's Brown Beauty' are hardy to Zone 6. These offer their large, lustrous leaves and striking form to the winter garden. The flowers of witch hazel are reflected beautifully in the glossy, mirror-finished leaves of the Southern magnolia when they're planted together. These hardier southern magnolias are best suited to being planted in protected garden sites on Cape Cod, in the warmer city environment of Providence,

Rhode Island, or in the more benign climate of what we call "the banana belt" along the south coast of New England.

OAK

The evergreen bamboo oak (*Quercus myrsinifolia*) is one more broadleaf evergreen tree with spectacular wintertime foliage. It merits a gardener's lust, especially to those practicing hardiness zone denial. It is hardy as far north as the Philadelphia region and is listed as a recommended evergreen tree for the Portland, Oregon area.

EVERGREENS FOR COLOR INTEREST

Evergreens with foliage colors *other* than green are significant to consider when designing and planting the winter garden. Chartreuse, chrome, golden yellow, silvery blue, blue-green, bronze-red, and black-green are all found in the foliage of conifers, as well as a few broadleaf plants. The study of the impact of color on the garden is as important as the analysis of the light-reflecting qualities and textures of green leaf surfaces that we looked at in the previous section.

Quercus myrsinifolia

While blue spruce (*Picea pungens* 'Glauca') is often placed as a lone specimen tree, its impact is doubled when placed for color interest.

BLUE HUES

The condition and quality of winter sunlight within the context of the season's bleakness change the circumstances and perception of color, reversing a basic premise in color theory that blue is a cool color that recedes. The winter landscape transforms blue foliage into lightness and warmth. As an example, the glaucous blue foliage of Colorado blue spruce (*Picea pungens* 'Glauca') doesn't recede in association with other green-needled conifers, but instead, in the light of winter atmosphere and surroundings, it projects a reflective warmth. In summertime, when the color green envelops and predominates the character of the landscape with illumination under a hot sun, the perception of the color blue shifts to a cool shadow.

The boughs of Colorado blue spruce may be considered commonplace and overfamiliar in American gardens, yet when seen with fresh eyes in their native environs, they are always striking—an impressive

The red fruits of *Malus* ×'Louisa' enhance the blue background tones of *Picea pungens* 'Montgomery'.

and unusual form. In the winter landscape of New England and for a large section of North America, they feel captivatingly exotic. Colorado spruce is native to the extraordinarily high-elevation landscape of the central Rocky Mountain states of Montana, Colorado, and New Mexico, though the blue-colored variant 'Glauca' is limited in the wild. It is a large, green, pyramidal conifer, hardy to Zone 2. The surface of its needles is covered in a waxy coating that creates its distinctive and much desired silver blue hue. Charles Parry collected cones and seeds of this blue form on Pikes Peak and sent them to the Arnold Arboretum in Boston in 1874; the progeny of these seeds are some of the oldest trees in the arboretum's conifer collection. Seed-grown plants are variable in color and result in gradient shades of blue-green.

The most glaucous blue selections, like *Picea pungens* 'Hoopsii', are propagated asexually by grafting. Many choice dwarf and weeping forms of Colorado blue spruce have been selected and propagated. They are well suited for smaller gardens where a fifty-foot tree will not fit. Electric blue needles clothe 'Glauca Procumbens', which scrambles along the ground. The compact, silver-blue 'Montgomery' is a choice cultivar that grows into a layered, six-foot mound. This dwarf form has a prominent history: It was selected by Colonel R. H. Montgomery at his Cos Cob, Connecticut estate and pinetum in the 1930s. He later donated this estate to the town of Greenwich and his conifer collection to the New York Botanical Garden in the Bronx. NYBG raised this plant and named it in Montgomery's honor.

The dwarf conifer collection at the Arnold Arboretum in Boston also includes many fine specimens. 'Hunnewelliana' is a rounded dwarf form with

Low-growing *Picea pungens* 'Glauca Procumbens' practically functions as a groundcover.

Picea pungens 'Montgomery' has a low, mounding habit.

Picea pungens 'Hoopsii'

Picea pungens 'Hunnewelliana' has a friendly, rotund form.

silver-blue foliage. It originated not far from Boston, at the Hunnewell Pinetum, as a seedling that was selected in the early 1920s.

White fir (*Abies concolor*), or concolor fir, is another coniferous inhabitant of mountainous slopes in the Rocky Mountains and southern Cascades, and a beautiful conical tree with distinct silver-blue foliage cast that can be used to anchor the background of the winter garden. It can withstand Zone 4 temperatures and in the wild may grow to a height of one hundred feet. Its gray-green needles are soft and flattened, in contrast to the Colorado blue spruce's sharp and angular ones. It is often grown as a cut Christmas tree.

SUBTLE SILVER

Silver is the most light-reflective metallic color. Silver-gray-green foliage is a pleasing and relaxing color in the garden, distinct from the blues described. It is a shade of green that doesn't impart any warm yellow tones. In a sense, this color of green is an abstract anomaly of a binary color that appears to be deficient in one of its principal components. Any yellow is masked under a silver bloom.

Take a look at the lacy, silvery foliage of *Cupressus arizonica* var. *glabra* 'Blue Ice' that shimmers and draws the eye like a magnet. The spiral arrangement of its waxy silver-blue, scale-like needles glistens and

Sequoiadendron giganteum 'Hazel Smith' is an exceptionally hardy blue form of giant sequoia. This cultivar was named in honor of the co-owner of Watnong Nurseries in Morris Plains, New Jersey. It was a solo seedling from Oregon that survived a New Jersey winter sometime around 1960. It can withstand Zone 5 temperatures.

Include *Cupressus arizonica* var. *glabra* 'Blue Ice' (top) in a planting paired with similar silver and blue-gray foliage, such as *Calluna vulgaris* 'Silver Knight' (above left), *Juniperus squamata* 'Blue Star' (above center), and *Salvia officinalis* 'Berggarten' (above right). Color repetition ameliorates the singularity of 'Blue Ice'.

sparkles. It is an unusual form of Arizona cypress discovered as a chance seedling in a New Zealand nursery! The parent species is found in the United States in New Mexico and Arizona, with its range extending into northern Mexico. *Cupressus arizonica* is hardy to Zones 7–8, with the variety *glabra* being hardier, to Zone 6. Its form is that of a compact and columnar small tree. Be careful not to use too many contrasting foliage colors with 'Blue Ice', as it can make a garish composition.

The Korean fir (*Abies koreana*) is native to the mountains of South Korea. It is a pyramidal evergreen with short, broad dark green needles that are silver on their underside. A very distinctive cultivar was introduced

Abies koreana 'Horstmann's Silberlocke'

Cedrus atlantica 'Glauca'

in 1979 by Gunther Horstmann of Schneverdeingen, Germany. Called 'Horstmann's Silberlocke', its needles curve up to display their exceptionally silver-white undersides. The German translation of its name is apt, meaning "silver locks of hair." It can withstand Zone 4 temperatures, and I have combined its silvery pyramidal form with the glossy foliage of American holly (*Ilex opaca*).

Blue Atlas cedar (*Cedrus atlantica* 'Glauca') hails from the Atlas Mountains in Algeria and Morocco in northwest Africa. Its bristly tufts of glaucous needles vie with Colorado blue spruce for the most intense blue, though they lean more to the silver end of the spectrum, and its form and texture are totally different. It is stiffly pyramidal with horizontal branches and becomes flat-topped with age. The weeping form (*Cedrus atlantica* 'Glauca Pendula'), by contrast, has long, pendant branches. It doesn't develop a strong vertical leader and will creep along the ground unless staked or trained to a structure. 'Glauca Pendula' makes a

Cedrus atlantica 'Glauca Pendula'

Cedrus libani ssp. *stenocoma* develops a flattened crown.

striking sculptural display when its blue curtain of cascading branches is draped over an arbor.

The hardy form of cedar of Lebanon (*Cedrus libani* ssp. *stenocoma*) originates from a northern population growing high in the Taurus Mountains in Turkey.

Charles Sargent, onetime director of the Arnold Arboretum in Boston, arranged for the seed to be collected, and they arrived at the arboretum in February 1902. This cedar is hardy in Zone 5. Its spreading horizontal branches are clothed in fine silver-gray needles. Venerable old trees develop a picturesque, flattened, umbelliform crown.

The Cypriot cedar (*Cedrus brevifolia*) is only found on the island of Cyprus and is hardy to Zone 6. A common synonym in some botanical references is

Cedrus libani var. *brevifolia*. Its stiffly branched open form is outlined with very short glaucous needles. *Cedrus deodara*, on the other hand, is distinguished by its long needles and drooping branches. It is hardy to Zones 7–8 and is not seen in gardens much north of Philadelphia. The cultivar 'Kashmir' has blue-green pendulous branchlets.

The blue-needled form of Japanese white pine (*Pinus parviflora* f. *glauca*) has long been cultivated in Japanese gardens. Its slightly twisted blue-green needles, striped with a white band on their underside, are arranged in bundles of five. It appears silvery thanks to these two-tone needles. The horizontal, branched silhouette of Japanese white pine echoes the mature, picturesque profile of eastern white pine (*Pinus strobus*), on a greatly reduced scale.

'Keteleeri' Chinese juniper (*Juniperus chinensis* 'Keteleeri') has glaucous foliage and showy, large, blueberry-like cones. It grows to be a small pyramidal

Juniperus chinensis 'Keteleeri'

Pinus parviflora f. *glauca*

Juniperus virginiana 'Grey Owl'

tree. *Juniperus virginiana* 'Grey Owl' is a unique spreading form of red cedar with silver-gray foliage. It is an interspecific triploid hybrid seedling of *Juniperus virginiana* 'Glauca' and *Juniperus* × 'Pfitzeriana' (itself a hybrid of *Juniperus chinensis* and *Juniperus sabina*) that originated in 1938 at the Caam Brothers Nursery in Oudenbosch, Netherlands. 'Grey Owl' was introduced in 1949 by F. J. Grootendorst & Sons Nursery in Boskoop, Netherlands. It is a female clone and produces highly ornamental blueberry-like cones in abundance. My twenty-five-year-old specimen is layered with silver-gray arching branches that span thirty feet across. It billows to a height of five feet.

Juniperus squamata 'Blue Star' is a diminutive cushion of silver-blue, awl-shaped needles. In spite of its name, white bands on the finely textured leaves make them gleam in the sun. 'Blue Star' is a dwarf branch sport of *Juniperus squamata* 'Meyeri' introduced in 1964 by Hoogeveen Nursery, Netherlands. It maintains its rich azure foliage color throughout the winter, becoming slightly more silver.

BRILLIANT YELLOW

Whatever your feelings about yellow, it does predominate in the landscape: It is the color of sunlight. The color yellow reverberates and is visually powerful and emphatic. It physically and spatially augments form. Yellow's glow makes it feel assertive and demanding of attention. The paint color chrome yellow was formulated in 1939 and designed to stand out at a glance, even in peripheral vision, specifically with school buses in mind. You simply can't ignore it. The foliage of some golden yellow conifers shares this same striking visual impact.

Juniperus squamata 'Blue Star'

A group of golden threadleaf cypress (*Chamaecyparis pisifera filifera* 'Aurea') has about the same impact in this landscape as that of a school bus parked at the base of the stone stairs.

In wintertime, many coniferous evergreens have foliage that changes hue slightly. Some take on a very different coloration with the onset of cold temperatures. Yellow's boldness must be taken in stride within the visual context and tones of the surrounding landscape. In a bodacious use of purposefully incendiary color, I planted a pair of the golden-foliaged 'Ogon' dawn redwoods (*Metasequoia glyptostroboides* 'Ogon') in front of a barn that had been painted hot chili pepper-red. The pair are accompanied by the fiery foliage of *Cotinus coggygria* 'Royal Purple', *Cotinus coggygria* 'Golden Spirit', *Spiraea thunbergi* 'Ogon', *Rosa glauca*, *Weigela florida* 'Rubidor', *Buddleia alternifolia* 'Argentea', *Elaeagnus* ×'Quicksilver', *Rhododendron* ×'Millennium', *Chamaecyparis obtusa* 'Crippsii', and *Abies concolor* 'Candicans'. This eye-popping planting of outrageously colored trees and shrubs is situated on a large property at the edge of a green field and a stand of mature white pines. Though many of the plants have deciduous leaves, the winter aspect of the vermillion-red barn is bolstered by the silver and gold duo of conifers and the naked boles of the dawn redwoods.

In the winter garden, yellow foliage radiates like shafts of sunlight and warms the frozen landscape. Personally, I find some golden yellow foliage more attractive than others. I discern either pleasure or distaste based on the association of leaf color, form, and texture interacting with light. In full sun, the gold thread-like sprays of *Chamaecyparis pisifera filifera* 'Aurea' appear brassy and present a harsh coarseness. However, when grown in partial shade, this color is muted to a pleasing chartreuse hue.

Chartreuse is an intermediate color between green and yellow. Horticulturally, it is a color reminiscent of fresh emerging leaves in spring. Landscape designers love to use chartreuse to make elegant color juxtapositions in the garden. In a collection of conifers at the Polly Hill Arboretum on Martha's Vineyard, the yellow foliage of *Chamaecyparis pisifera filifera* 'Aurea' takes on more of a chartreuse glowing pool of light in contrast to the dark foliage of the adjacent *Chamaecyparis obtusa* 'Coralliformis'.

Golden yellow as a color is most becoming when it is displayed on the flat, frond-like foliage of a conifer such as *Chamaecyparis obtusa* 'Crippsii' or *Thuja*

Chamaecyparis pisifera filifera 'Aurea', grown in partial shade, takes on a chartreuse hue and complements the darker foliage of *Chamaecyparis obtusa* 'Coraliformis'.

Thuja occidentalis 'Lutea'

occidentalis 'Lutea', Light and shadow transform this leaf form into precious filigree. Commonly known as George Peabody arborvitae, *Thuja occidentalis* 'Lutea' is an old but sound cultivar introduced to gardens in 1881. Its ferny foliage is held in a vertical orientation, and light and shadow striking it divides its surfaces into deep color gradations. In 1987, I transplanted a sixteen-foot-tall specimen into a new garden at Tranquil Lake Nursery; after thirty-four years, it towers more than forty feet tall, with a spread at its base of twenty-five feet, and is one of several conifers that form the bones of the garden. Its golden foliage adds a glowing presence of light to the garden year-round.

Chamaecyparis obtusa 'Crippsii' is a classic golden-foliage form of the Japanese Hinoki false cypress. The British nursery Thomas Cripps & Son raised and distributed this cultivar in 1901. It will slowly grow to a small, loosely conical tree, and the horizontal aspect of its broad, frond-like, golden yellow branchlets helps differentiate it immediately from arborvitae. 'Crippsii' will thrive both in a full-sun garden or in a shady understory. The foliage turns chartreuse in the shade.

Chamaecyparis obtusa 'Crippsii'

Thuja occidentalis 'Rheingold'

Thuja occidentalis 'Ellwangeriana Aurea' is named for the acclaimed Rochester, New York nurseryman George Ellwanger, who raised and introduced this beautiful chartreuse-colored arborvitae in 1875. The names 'Ellwangerian Aurea' and 'Rheingold' are conflated in botanical nomenclature, but 'Rheingold' is a dwarf form of arborvitae with juvenile, awl-shaped leaves. Like some conifer sports, this cultivar has unstable new growth—the foliage freely reverts from its awl needles to mature scale-like foliage. Without vigilant pruning, 'Rheingold' will eventually revert and grow to become 'Ellwangeriana Aurea'. Some photographic encyclopedia references identify a mature leaf-form conifer as 'Rheingold'. Regardless of this characteristic confusion, 'Ellwangerian Aurea' is a compact-growing,

chartreuse-colored shrub whose foliage has rose tints in summer and a warm amber color in winter; try pairing it with the chartreuse-colored stems of the variegated yellow twig dogwood (*Cornus sericea* 'Silver and Gold').

In a playfully designed garden at Tranquil Lake Nursery, I painted twelve-foot-tall cut bamboo culms a brilliant yellow. They stand in a close-spaced random arrangement in three clusters that form a linear axis through the center of a garden. Twelve-inch diameter, ten-foot-tall PVC columns painted violet flank the perimeter. The yellow bamboo rods arise from a planting of the evergreen golden foliage of Japanese sweet flag (*Acorus gramineus* 'Ogon'). The yellow groundcover substantially magnifies the visual presence of

Painted yellow bamboo culms function as sculpture in summer at Tranquil Lake Nursery and inject vibrant color in winter (left), when the yellow is echoed by *Pinus virginiana* 'Wate's Golden' (right).

the thin bamboo rods. This exaggeration is illusionary; the paint color doesn't tangibly change the size of the bamboo. However, the transformative impact of color is real, making them into luminous shafts of light. The yellow paint color is echoed in the golden winter foliage of *Pinus virginiana* 'Wate's Golden' grown in a container.

The Virginia pine (*Pinus virginiana*) of the southern United States is analogous to the jack pine (*Pinus banksiana*) found in the north. Both are scrubby trees that grow in barren habitats with infertile soils.

Pinus virginiana 'Wate's Golden' is an outstanding selection for the winter garden. Its lime-green needles transform to golden yellow with cold temperatures. Growing it in a permanent container so roots are more exposed to cold air temperatures intensifies its needle color. This unusual chameleon cultivar originated sometime in the 1960s as a sport seedling and can withstand Zone 4 temperatures.

Dragon's eye Japanese red pine (*Pinus densiflora* 'Oculus-draconis') presents a novel needle coloration pattern: Its needles are marked with two yellow

Pinus virginiana 'Wate's Golden' in full winter needle color and tinted with frost

bands. When viewed radially from the terminal bud, the golden color forms a pattern of concentric rings, resembling an "eye" in the green needles. Overall, its color impression in the winter landscape is a glowing golden yellow. This unique Japanese pine grows into an open-branched, twenty-five-foot-tall tree with distinctive cinnamon orange bark. It is hardy to Zone 4. More diminutive in size and forming a small, shrubby tree is *Pinus parviflora* 'Ogon Janome', This form of Japanese white pine with gold-banded needles is hardy to Zone 5.

Oriental spruce (*Picea orientalis*) has exceedingly short, lustrous, dark-green needles that clothe a pyramidal structure. It is the finest-textured spruce and tolerates partial shade. 'Skylands' is a gold-leaf cultivar found as a random seedling at the New Jersey Botanical Garden at Skylands in Ringwood, New Jersey. Its refined, shining-gold silhouette brightens the winter landscape.

BRONZES AND BROWNS

While botanical literature and plant descriptions written by nurseries may euphemistically describe the color change of some needles as "reddish bronze" or "purple brown," simply stated, that means the foliage changes to the color of rust. This is not to say it is unattractive. *Juniperus virginiana*, *Cryptomeria japonica*, and *Microbiota decussata* have foliage that changes to a rust-colored winter complexion.

Eastern red cedar (*Juniperus virginiana*) is the most widely distributed coniferous tree in the continental United States. Its native territory extends from southern Maine to northwest Florida and west from North Dakota to Texas. It is found in diverse habitats that range from the edges of tidal salt marshes to infertile

The bicolor striped needles and cinnamon-colored bark of *Pinus densiflora* 'Oculus-draconis' make it a dramatic focal point in any garden.

Pinus parviflora 'Ogon Janome'

Juniperus virginiana

Juniperus virginiana 'Burkii' leaflets in winter

abandoned fields and pastures, which it colonizes readily. Red cedar's juvenile leaves are like needles, whereas mature leaves are like scales. These are arranged into opposite overlapping pairs, and branches will often exhibit both leaf types. Eastern red cedar forms a pyramidal tree growing from thirty to fifty feet tall. *Juniperus virginiana* 'Burkii' is a compact cultivar, growing to twenty feet with glaucous summer foliage that turns purple-brown in winter.

Japanese cedar (*Cryptomeria japonica*) is a large coniferous tree hardy to Zone 5. This tree's leaves are awl-shaped needles, and they cover branchlets densely, in a spiral arrangement. Young trees have a narrow form with ascending branches. A mature Japanese cedar develops a picturesque, openly branched crown of tufted foliage. This tasseled appearance makes its profile easily recognizable from a distance, especially in winter, when its foliage turns a distinctive bronze color. Japanese cedar's foliage color and texture give spatial depth to a border when combined with other evergreen trees. It also comes in many dwarf forms. The cultivar 'Mushroom' forms a fluffy bun of juvenile awl-shaped foliage whose warm bronze color is welcome in winter.

Russian arborvitae (*Microbiota decussata*) is native to the Siberian mountains. It is a spreading procumbent shrub displaying a dense carpet of feathery, fan-like leaves arranged in flat sprays similar to arborvitae. In winter, its matte green foliage changes to bronze. Russian arborvitae will grow in the sun or shade and is effective as a companion to glossy leaved sweetbox (*Sarcococca hookeriana* var. *humilis*) or conversely as a foil to *Yucca filamentosa* 'Golden Sword', *Picea pungens* 'Baby Blueeyes', *Lindera angustifolia*, or *Acer griseum*.

Cryptomeria japonica 'Elegans Compacta' bronzed up and ready for winter

Cryptomeria japonica 'Mushroom'

Cryptomeria japonica 'Lobbii'

Microbiota decussata

BORDERING ON BLACK

The black-green foliage of the genus *Taxus*, commonly called yew, stands apart from other evergreens. If conifer foliage color was analogous to fabric, yew has the eminence of bearing suitable for fashioning formal attire. However, this elegantly clad conifer has fallen out of style since its heyday more than half a century ago. In the 1970s, nursery catalogs listed dozens of different cultivars with a variety of growth habits, from prostrate to narrowly upright. I remember nursery fields planted with hundreds of acres of yews in Rhode Island and the fertile Connecticut River Valley, north of Hartford. In my early horticultural career, I hand pruned thousands of linear feet of yew hedges that lined the elevated perimeter of Constitution Plaza in downtown Hartford, Connecticut—with a pair of classic Seymour-Smith hand shears! There are several probable reasons for the decline in popularity of yew. Deer browsing is one—only urban landscapes isolated from deer populations are safe from devastation. Yew's ubiquity in residential plantings may also be a contributing factor. The practice of unskilled, or inept, horticultural pruning has also damaged the perception of yew in the garden. Too often, this elegant conifer is sheared into disconcerting shapes in mundane landscapes.

Japanese yew (*Taxus cuspidata*) is native to Korea, China, Russia, and Japan. In its native habitat, it can grow to be a thirty- to fifty-foot tree with reddish brown bark. It is dioecious; female plants produce a fleshy, red, fruit-like aril around a single seed. The dark green leaves form flat, lanceolate-shaped needles. It can withstand Zone 4 temperatures. *Taxus cuspidata* 'Capitata' has a more pyramidal form and, when grown with a single trunk, becomes a substantial tree. English yew (*Taxus baccata*) is native to Europe and hardy to Zone 6. It is a venerable and long-lived evergreen tree. The Ankerwycke Yew grows in a meadow on the banks of the River Thames near Windsor, England—experts on ancient trees have estimated that it is well over 2000 years old. It has a girth of over 29 and a half feet! A hybrid cross of *Taxus cuspidata* and *Taxus baccata* was recorded around 1900. It was made by horticulturist T. D. Hatfield at the Hunnewell Pinetum in Wellesley, Massachusetts, resulting in *Taxus ×media*. At about the same time, Long Island, New York nurseryman Henry Hicks

Taxus cuspidata features very dark needles over reddish brown bark.

made a similar specific cross that was named *Taxus ×media* 'Hicksii'. These hybrid progeny are cold hardy to Zone 4.

The spreading English yew (*Taxus baccata* 'Repandens') was introduced in the late 1880s by Samuel Parsons & Sons Nursery in Flushing, New York. It is hardy to Zone 5, more tolerant of cold than the species. Its black-green leaves and loose procumbent habit make it one of the most elegant of winter conifers. Another spreader is Japanese plum yew (*Cephalotaxus harringtonia* 'Prostrata'). It is similar in form, though its glossy needles are larger. It will tolerate the heat and humidity of the south and is hardy in Zones 6 to 9. *Cephalotaxus* is also shade tolerant, but most important, it is distasteful to deer.

GREENING THE GROUND PLANE

Winter's cold temperatures and desiccating winds diminish the verdant color of the summertime greensward to a dull tan. Though a white blanket of snow can offer aesthetic relief, it is not consistent or reliable. Prostrate and creeping forms of conifers are ideal for adding a vital and ever-present green to the winter garden.

Taxus ×media 'Hicksii' has become popular as a hedging plant in many gardens.

Loosely spreading boughs give *Taxus baccata* 'Repandens' a distinguished air.

Cephalotaxus harringtonii 'Prostrata'

Creeping juniper (*Juniperus horizontalis*) is a prostrate, ground-hugging evergreen conifer that flourishes in full sun, and it is an excellent evergreen alternative to turf grass in some garden settings. Its spread is transcontinental! Creeping juniper grows in a variety of habitats throughout Canada, from Labrador and Newfoundland to Yukon and northern British Columbia. It can withstand Zone 2 temperatures. It is also native to New England and in sunny habitats west to the Great Lakes. The *Royal Horticultural Society Encyclopedia of Conifers,* published in 2013, lists ninety-six different cultivars of *Juniperus horizontalis* alone!

Juniperus horizontalis 'Wiltonii' has a very flat form with distinctive blue foliage. It was collected on the Penobscot Bay island of Vinalhaven, Maine in 1914. Try pairing it with the gold foliage of a sumac with the trade name Tiger Eyes (*Rhus typhina* 'Bailtiger').

Along the granite-bound coast of Maine, tough creeping juniper is found in niches between fractured ledges, knitting the seaside landscape together with its evergreen foliage. It is pictured here with winter-red *Empetrum nigrum*.

Another popular mat-forming juniper, *Juniperus horizontalis* 'Bar Harbor', was propagated and introduced in 1939 from a plant found on Mount Desert Island, Maine. It has glaucous gray-green foliage. 'Bar Harbor' does require space to grow: A single plant will easily extend to a diameter spread of ten feet across, so it is not a plant suitable for a narrow three-foot-wide border. A group of *Juniper horizontalis* 'Bar Harbor' has the potential to cover several thousand square feet. It will make an attractive, evergreen, drought-tolerant, and low-maintenance ground cover.

Juniperus horizontalis 'Douglasii' has a rougher texture and grows slightly taller than 'Bar Harbor'. I have used it as an evergreen foreground in a border planted with the reddish winter stems of lowbush blueberry (*Vaccinium angustifolium*), the red fruit of red-bud crab apple (*Malus ×zumi* var. *calocarpa*), inkberry holly (*Ilex glabra* 'Compacta'), and cutleaf staghorn sumac (*Rhus typhina* 'Laciniata') next to Serbian spruce (*Picea omorika*).

The larger spreading junipers in the Pfitzer group grow to be beautiful, very broad shrubs. At Tranquil Lake Nursery, a fifty-year-old specimen of *Juniperus ×pfitzeriana* 'Aurea' is fifty feet across! It is a billowing two- to three-foot-high wave of arching foliage that surges to a height of five feet in its center.

Dwarf and unusual forms of conifers fit into a wide range of gardens. They can stand in for sculptures and are especially effective in the winter garden. Their slow growth rate and diminutive stature make them appear as unchanging forms in the landscape. Of course, "dwarf" is a relative term. Plants that grow less than three inches per year are considered miniature forms. These may only mature to three feet high over fifteen years. Other conifers, somewhat larger but still

Juniperus ×pfitzeriana 'Pfitzeriana Aurea' is impressive, but it's not a plant suitable for a small garden.

LEFT *Abies koreana* 'Aurea' displays golden needles that gleam with polished silver undersides.

BELOW At the Conetown Pinetum of Bedrock Gardens in Lee, New Hampshire, the chartreuse foliage of *Chamaecyparis obtusa* 'Goldilocks' is in direct contrast to the glossy green whorls of *Sciadopitys verticillata* 'Joe Kozy' and the fine dark green needles of *Picea orientalis* 'Compacta'.

dwarf, may grow three to six inches or more annually. Dwarf conifer variants may originate as random seedlings or from propagating a branch mutation that develops very congested growth, which is known as a witches' broom.

There are notable collections of dwarf conifers in many arboreta and botanic gardens. Many feature a montage arrangement of plants that blend their various distinct forms and colors. The snake branch spruce (*Picea abies* 'Virgata') is a favorite at many due to its unusual appearance. Its long, contorted, whip-like green-needled shoots are sparsely branched. Its form is somewhat chaotic, with some branches pendulous and others curving upward. Likewise, an exceedingly fine specimen of *Tsuga caroliniana* 'La Bar's Weeping' will present a dramatic, horizontally weeping profile. The embracing sculptural form of its evergreen branches imparts a memorable greeting to garden guests. But these specimens should hardly be relgated to specialty gardens; if the whimiscial nature of one or another strikes you, plant one in your own yard where visitors

Picea abies 'Virgata', the aptly named snake branch spruce

Tsuga canadensis 'Sargentii'

will happen upon it unexpectedly, or site it in a special spot just for yourself.

In gardens restricted to small spaces, choosing a dwarf conifer that won't grow too large is key, oxymoronic as that may sound. A choice plant should be positioned prominently, perhaps to be viewed in an entry garden or through a window. When selecting plants for small, intimate spaces, it is also important to consider a color theme. Combining many different colored forms of foliage in a small garden creates an abrupt contrast and can feel unsettled or uncomfortable on a subconscious level. Such a riotous celebration of color and texture may be most effective in large, open spaces.

One stalwart of the dwarf category for home gardens is the dwarf Alberta spruce (*Picea glauca* 'Conica'). Though now very common, this small tree has a rare and distinctive lineage. It was discovered by two elite horticulturalists, John G. Jack and Alfred Rehder, dendrologists from the Arnold Arboretum in Boston. They fortuitously found and collected this dwarf form of white spruce in Alberta, Canada as they were botanizing along the railway tracks while they waited for a train back to Boston.

The dwarf Alberta spruce may be the most commercially successful and popular dwarf conifer ever introduced. It is ubiquitous in both residential and commercial landscapes—and for that has nearly become cliché. I find that a dwarf Alberta spruce is almost always in one's peripheral vision! Unfortunately, this classic dwarf conifer is often planted in an amusing, though plebeian fashion. It can be found in cemeteries, flanking tombstones, or just as frequently, planted too close to residential entrances or at the corners of houses. To borrow and paraphrase a paradoxical witticism from baseball great Yogi Berra, anything that is popular is bound to be disliked. I have to deliberately remind myself of the beautiful qualities of *Picea glauca* 'Conica'. I still remember being mesmerized in my first encounter with it, over fifty years ago. A majestic mature pair flanked stone steps at Thuya Garden in Northeast Harbor, Maine.

Their fine-textured moss green foliage revealed an elegant pyramidal uniformity. These original specimens had even been transplanted from Beatrix Farrand's Reef Point Estate in Bar Harbor in 1958. In spite of being charmed so many years ago, I am guilty of infrequently planting dwarf Alberta spruce in gardens today. Recently, however, I planted it in a new garden at Tranquil Lake Nursery to once again celebrate its conical, mossy green mien—and I should note that another at the nursery has thrived in a permanent thirty-six-inch diameter container since 1988. (More on that in the chapter Planting Permanent Pots.)

Weeping conifers have shapes that never fail to be novel and fanciful. Weeping white pine (*Pinus strobus* 'Pendula') forms a large, shaggy umbrella of ascending and arching branches with pendant foliage. *Pinus strobus* 'John's Find' is a unique pendulous form—it is a chance seedling of *Pinus strobus* cultivars 'Pendula' and 'Torulosa' found by John Nassif, production manager at Summer Hill Nursery in Madison, Connecticut.

LEFT A venerable containerized dwarf Alberta spruce (*Picea glauca* 'Conica') at Tranquil Lake Nursery

BELOW A weeping cultivar of *Tsuga canadensis*

'John's Find' is a compact grower with a horizontal armature and pendulous branches.

Perhaps the most famous weeping conifer is Sargent's weeping hemlock (*Tsuga canadensis* 'Sargentii'). In a 2020 article in in the Arnold Arboretum's *Arnoldia*, horticulturist Peter Del Tredici detailed a sleuth's story of the discovery of this unique weeping conifer around 1850 in New York. He explores various accounts of its establishment on Henry Winthrop Sargent's estate and its subsequent propagation and dissemination. This history traces the early propagated plants given to

Charles Sprague Sargent in Brookline, Massachusetts, and Horatio Hollis Hunnewell in Wellesley. Sargent's weeping hemlock forms a domed mound with its pendulous branches cascading like an emerald waterfall. In the trade, 'Sargentii' and other weeping hemlocks are often referred to as 'Pendula'.

A very dwarf form of Canadian hemlock is the cultivar 'Jervis'. Its tiny needles are tightly congested on the twigs. In 1988, I displayed a sizable specimen of 'Jervis' in a garden at the Massachusetts Horticultural Society's New England Spring Flower Show. That specimen, transplanted back into the gardens at Tranquil Lake Nursery, is now fifty years old. Growing no more than an inch a year, 'Jervis' is a beautiful, irregular, bonsai-like miniature tree. It now measures eight feet tall with a twelve-foot spread!

The creeping Norway spruce (*Picea abies* 'Repens') is another common dwarf conifer. It is squat and flat when young; after fifty years, 'Repens' acquires more personality in its form. It may reach an irregular spread of fifteen feet, with several domes of foliage that form a gradual height of four feet. The drooping Norway spruce (*Picea abies* 'Inversa'), on the other hand, romps along the ground, making a giant octopus-like shape. Its ascending branches undulate and form a weeping hummock of green branches. Similarly, both 'Prostrate Beauty' Korean fir (*Abies koreana* 'Prostrate Beauty') and 'Hillside Creeper' Scots pine (*Pinus sylvestris* 'Hillside Creeper') are dwarf and prostrate spreading cultivars of large forest trees. The layered foliage of the former shows off the white underside of its needles, while the latter forms a spreading mat of blue-green foliage.

Other prostrate pines include a procumbent form of pitch pine (*Pinus rigida* 'Sand Beach'), which can be found growing on granite ledges on Mount Desert

Slow-growing *Tsuga canadensis* 'Jervis'. When staked and trained, the weeping Norway spruce (*Picea abies* 'Pendula') is an ideal plant to frame a garden entry. Its arching form and pendulous branches make a curtain of green foliage that embraces an arbor gate. The form of *Picea abies* 'Pendula' is variable; a specimen at the Arnold Arboretum presents as a vertical shaft of pendant branches.

Picea abies 'Pendula'

Picea abies 'Repens'

Pinus rigida 'Sand Beach'

Pinus banksiana 'Schoodic'

Island, Maine; *Pinus banksiana* 'Schoodic', a form of jack pine, from seed collected at Schoodic peninsula in Maine by Al Fordham of the Arnold Arboretum; and *Pinus parviflora* 'Adcock's Dwarf', a tiny needled, slow-growing gem of Japanese white pine. It was raised in 1961 by Graham Adcock at Hillier Nurseries in England, and its irregular branched form is clad with gray green needles. Prominently placed on the edge of a stone terrace, it mimics a bonsai growing in a crack in a rock outcrop.

Pinus parviflora 'Adcock's Dwarf'

Many varieties of boxwood (*Buxus* species) have foliage that adds an invaluable evergreen component to the winter garden. Although boxwood can be pruned into a variety of shapes, its use should not be confined to hedges or limited to formally structured gardens. Left to grow naturally, many forms of boxwood create attractive greenery under wintry trees. I have used *Buxus sempervirens* 'Vardar Valley' as an effective green foil beneath the gray bark of star magnolia (*Magnolia stellata*), as well as the mottled bark of Persian ironwood (*Parrotia persica*). 'Vardar Valley' forms a flat-topped spreading shrub with distinctively rounded dark green leaves. Its new growth is flushed a bluish hue. It is hardy to Zone 4.

This significant and beautiful boxwood cultivar was introduced to the horticultural world through a circuitous and serendipitous path. In 1934, thirty-seven-year-old horticultural scholar and Arnold Arboretum arborist Edgar Anderson traveled to the Balkans on a plant-collecting expedition. The mountainous landscape he encountered along the tributaries of the Vardar River gorge was far from pristine—the forested hillsides were eroded and devastated by years of over-cutting and overgrazing. In his writings about the journey, Anderson referenced goats as one of the worst environmental offenders, as they devoured vast acres of boxwood, leaving some shrubs nibbled to the ground. He and his expedition collected seeds and botanical specimens, as well as four *Buxus sempervirens* cuttings, two from a wild source, and sent them to London to be propagated by associates at the John Innes Horticultural Institution. In the following spring of 1935, the four rooted cuttings arrived at the Arnold Arboretum in Boston.

Buxus sempervirens 'Vardar Valley'

Buxus sinica var. *insularis* 'Tide Hill'

Combine 'Tide Hill' boxwood with the contrasting glaucous blue needles of Japanese white pine (*Pinus parviflora* f. 'Glauca').

Edgar Anderson left the arboretum after the Balkan trip, and his horticultural career led him to become the director of the Missouri Botanical Garden, followed by a return to his passions of teaching and research. His Balkan boxwood accessions, however, were subsequently propagated and distributed to other horticultural institutions. After twenty-three years, in 1957, Arnold Arboretum horticulturist Donald Wyman named one of Anderson's Balkan boxwoods 'Vardar Valley'. A superlative cultivar, it exhibits outstanding winter hardiness and that unique, flat-topped spreading form. It has also proved resistant to boxwood blight and deer browsing, and its natural "wild" growth form adds unique beauty to the winter landscape.

A cultivar of the Korean littleleaf boxwood, *Buxus sinica* var. *insularis* 'Tide Hill', also has a natural spreading and mounding habit, though much more diminutive than 'Vardar Valley'. 'Tide Hill' was named and introduced in 1954. Left unpruned, it grows a foot or so in height, with a spread of four feet. It makes a verdant, undulating base for planting under trees.

The best foliar pairings for keeping the garden alive with green in winter combine the textures of broadleaf and coniferous evergreen foliage. Perhaps the most effective strategy for incorporating these greens into the winter garden is to keep in mind the classic design principle of creating a harmony of contrasts. Use repetition for emphasis and focus in using evergreens while being aware that too many of the same may make a garden boring and dull. Instead, celebrate the winter garden with a vibrant mixture of many shades and textures of green.

Form and structure in a garden that mixes conifers and deciduous species at the Bressingham Gardens, designed by Adrian Bloom

Chapter Three

Marcescent Foliage

W hat is more captivating and beautiful in the dead of winter than a backlit hillside grove of American beech (*Fagus grandifolia*), with their winter leaves illuminated in a translucent, warm, coppery glow? "Marcescence" refers to the characteristic of some temperate woody plants to retain their dead or withered leaves firmly affixed to their stalks, or petioles, through winter. It is a botanical enigma. It may also seem peculiar to describe these pallid, hanging dried leaves as a superlative or desirable feature. Yet their appeal in a winter garden, when used as an intentional design element, is undeniable.

The aesthetic attributes of plants are strongly influenced by the abstract interplay of color and light. The quality or angle of light also markedly affects the experience of a garden and landscape. Think of exploring the desert landscapes of Arizona and Utah during the month of August; it may seem an exercise in counterintuitiveness to compare a freezing winter landscape to a sweltering desert one, but the

Herringbone-veined beech leaves create just enough texture to allow snow to stick to them beguilingly.

intense southwestern sun renders the desert's serene sparseness beautiful. It also illuminates the geological features of the landscape and the spiny and succulent plants that live under its harsh brutality. The essence of beauty is contradistinction.

American beech (*Fagus grandifolia*) is the standard-bearer for trees with marcescent foliage, and its winter character is more substantive than simply a change in color from green summer leafiness. Beech leaves are ovate in shape with serrated margins. They are five to six inches long and half as wide. Their bilaterally symmetrical herringbone-patterned venation becomes more pronounced in its winter guise.

This sequential arrangement of leaf veins produces a slightly ruffled surface texture, which adds reflective facets to the leaves' surfaces and makes them highly reflective, gleaming in the winter sun. The result of this alchemical transformation is a fundamental change in the aesthetic spirit of the American beech tree over the seasons.

American beech is a large tree that can grow to sixty feet in height and spread. However, it is also very amenable to pruning and can be maintained as

American beech is easily trained into hedge form.

The deeply lobed leaves of *Quercus alba* stand out starkly against a winter landscape.

a six-foot-high clipped hedge. Beech's marcescent foliage should be as celebrated in winter as the glossy green leaves of holly.

Oaks share a botanical relationship to beeches, as both are members of the Fagaceae family, so it is not surprising that some also express the marcescent foliage trait. The distinctive, deeply incised, lobed leaves of white oak (*Quercus alba*) are noted for hanging on branches in defiance of winter. Their foliage turns to a dark khaki-tan color that accentuates this lobed venation. The degree to which oaks retain their leaves can vary from year to year. Persistent foliage seems to develop mostly on juvenile growth.

The hornbeam maple (*Acer carpinifolium*) shows consistent marcescent qualities in my Massachusetts garden. This foliage characteristic is not found in botanical references. Juvenile growth and environmental conditions may be factors in its leaf retention.

It is growing in the shade of a large yellowwood tree (*Cladrastis kentukea*), with *Lindera angustifolia* nearby.

The most outstanding example of marcescent winter foliage is Asian spicebush (*Lindera angustifolia*). It is a multi-stemmed upright shrub that reaches ten feet in height, is hardy to Zone 5, and accommodates a range of cultural conditions. It thrives from full sun to partial shade and tolerates moist soils despite the fact that it is also very drought resistant. Four- to five-inch-long glossy, lanceolate leaves of olive green clothe its branches in summer. In autumn, its foliage turns an eye-catching pumpkin orange. By late November, as if by magic, the leaves are transformed to a gleaming copper. This beautifully marcescent winter foliage stands up to snow and inclement weather without the drop of a leaf. Foliage persists until the first week of May; then, as *Lindera angustifolia* unfurls

Leaves of *Lindera angustifolia* turn from orange in fall to bronze as winter progresses and persist on the plant even as new leaf buds emerge in spring.

clusters of tiny, bright yellow flowers at the leaf axils, the new leaf buds swell, and the long-sustained leaves drop. It is quite a feat, for essentially *Lindera angustifolia* is a shrub that has ever-bearing ornamental leaves.

This long virtuoso performance is accentuated when it is paired with broadleaf evergreen partners in the winter garden. Asian spicebush's smooth and simple leaf shape is even more stunning when positioned next to glossy dark-green toothed leaves of 'Jersey Princess'

holly (*Ilex opaca* 'Jersey Princess'). Combining it with the bold, pinnately compound, glossy leaves of *Mahonia bealei* and the tropical-looking foliage of yellow grove bamboo (*Phyllostachys aureosulcata*) creates an exceedingly captivating garden composition. The branched sprays of mahonia's golden-yellow flowers set against the glowing coppery warmth of *Lindera* leaves is the epitome of the beauty that marcescent leaves add to the winter garden.

Chapter Four

Ornamental Bark

Denuded of their foliage, deciduous trees and shrubs reveal their arboreal physique, a framework of trunks, branches, and twigs. In the winter landscape, the naked character of bark comes into prominent focus. Bark is the durable, fibrous cloak that wraps the stems of woody plants and functions as a barrier to damage. It also reduces water loss. Trees have evolved many distinctive decorative qualities of color and texture in their bark. Winter stems and trunks present a range of surfaces, from multicolored and mottled to peeling in sheer sheets and ribbons, and from exquisitely smooth to rough or deeply furrowed. The pigmented bark of some trees and shrubs becomes more vivid with exposure to winter's cold temperatures.

The most significant identifying characteristic of some trees is their superlative bark. Several different genera quickly come to mind as examples: *Betula*, *Acer*, and *Stewartia*. I would include any of them in a garden for their beautiful winter presence alone. Their green summer leaves, camellia-like flowers, and blazing fall foliage color are nice highlights, yet they

Betula nigra 'Heritage'

are ephemeral, and even superfluous, when compared to their trunks' permanent mien.

BIRCH

The caulk-white color and exfoliating bark of paper birch (*Betula papyrifera*) is unique among trees of northern forests. White phantoms of the woods, their luminous trunks glow in summer moonlight as well as dim winter sun. Paper birch's peeling white trunks are desirable for tactile engagement—a nuisance, perhaps, in public plantings, but arguably an attractive one nonetheless.

Canoe birch, another common name for *Betula papyrifera*, refers to its ethnobotanical use by the Indigenous Wabanaki people, a confederacy of American Indian nations who lived primarily in the New England states and parts of Atlantic Canada. They incorporated birch bark into their buildings, utilitarian objects, and as sheathing for canoes. This venerable birch-bark canoe craft has been kept alive by artisans working in the haunts where paper birch flourishes, from Maine to Michigan.

Paper birch grows to be a large tree, sixty feet or more in height. It has an erect branching habit that allows it to fit into relatively small landscape spaces. Paper birch is a native of cold climates, from Canada south through the New England states and west along the Great Lakes to Minnesota. Disjunct populations do endure farther south, but at high elevations and in the cooler climate of the Appalachian Mountains. An eighty-seven-foot-tall specimen in New Hampshire claimed the 2019 prize for size in the National Register of Champion Trees.

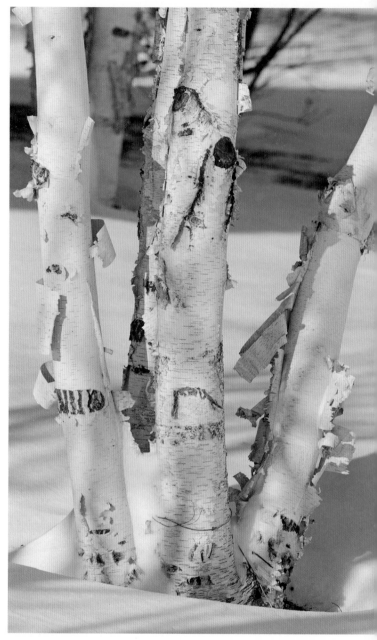

Betula papyrifera

The history of the utility of *Betula papyrifera* spans the gamut from aboriginal to modern, from being a provider of canoe skins to an element of avant-garde style. Perhaps the most recognizable landscape design of the twentieth century is of a hillside grove of paper birch: the iconic Blue Steps at Naumkeag, a public garden and historic home in Stockbridge, Massachusetts. It is a landscape masterpiece created by Fletcher Steele for Mabel Choate in 1938. Naumkeag is now under the care of The Trustees of Reservations.

The Blue Steps is a complex and dynamic design featuring forced perspectives. It is a modernist, monochromatic montage of white and dark. Shadowy, semicircular niches framed by pale concentric arcs are flanked by a series of steps, ramps, and swooping, round railings. This juxtaposing of light and shadow and repeating concave patterns and curved lines forms an uphill progression that bisects a grove of white-barked birches. Since its inception, Fletcher Steele's striking design continues to receive acclaim. May this grove of paper birches continue to live on to intrigue and inspire. The house and landscape of Naumkeag were originally designed as a summer retreat; however, the garden's distinct beauty throughout summer, fall, and into winter is not lost on visitors to the Berkshires.

Gray birch (*Betula populifolia*) is a tree of considerably lesser stature than paper birch. It grows in height to just twenty to thirty feet, a good fit in smaller landscapes. Gray birch has smooth, ash-white bark accented by black chevron patches at the branch collars. It is frequently found growing as a multiple-stemmed clump. Though often described as short-lived, gray birch has regenerative ability, sustaining itself by sprouting a succession of new stems.

Like paper birch, river birch (*Betula nigra*) also grows to be a large tree. However, it is much more heat and drought tolerant than paper birch. The native range of *Betula nigra* stretches well into southern climates; extending from southern New England to northern Florida, west to Texas and north to Minnesota along the Mississippi River. *Betula nigra* 'Cully', sold under the trade name Heritage, has peeling bark that is much lighter than the typical species. It is roughly ruffled and exfoliates in shades of white, tan, and salmon pink. Juvenile trees display bark that is quite white in color, darkening as the trunks age. This distinctive cultivar of river birch was first described in horticulture by nurseryman Earl Cully in St. Louis,

Betula nigra 'Cully'

Missouri. Heritage river birch has been widely planted due to its cultural tolerances and resistance to pests. The colorful bark of Heritage river birch is smashing in combination with winter-blooming witch hazels, such as *Hamamelis* ×'Diane' with orange-red flowers.

Betula nigra 'Little King' is a diminutive form of river birch that only attains a height of twenty feet. It is often grown as a multi-stemmed tree and has bark colorations similar to that of Heritage. 'Little King' develops into a fairly tightly branched and twiggy tree. It benefits from judicious pruning and

Betula nigra 'Little King'

Ilex opaca

Thuja occidentalis 'Lutea'

Buxus sempervirens 'Vardar Valley'

Dryopteris erythrosora 'Brilliance'

Ilex verticillata

The winter aspects of all of the light-barked birches are best set off by evergreen foliage. The verdant accent can be a background of broadleaf evergreen or coniferous trees such as American holly (*Ilex opaca*) or George Peabody arborvitae (*Thuja occidentalis* 'Lutea'), or add a green skirt of shade-tolerant shrubs such as *Leucothoe axillaris* or *Buxus sempervirens* 'Vardar Valley'. These combinations are just the basic beginning bones that create a vibrant winter garden. Accent with the red berries of winterberry holly (*Ilex verticillata*), the evergreen fronds of 'Brilliance' Japanese shield fern (*Dryopteris erythrosora* 'Brilliance'), the exfoliating orange-brown stems of oakleaf hydrangea (*Hydrangea quercifolia*), and the fragrant, bright yellow winter flowers of Chinese witch hazel (*Hamamelis mollis*) for an exuberant winter landscape.

Hamamelis mollis

thinning of its branches to best show off its physique, as well as to prevent lower branches from shading out and dying.

MAPLE

The maple family contains several species and cultivars with colorful winter trunks. Paperbark maple (*Acer griseum*) is one of the most attractive, endowed with peeling, cinnamon-red bark. It is native to central China and was collected and introduced to Boston's Arnold Arboretum by E. H. Wilson in 1907. The original accession has become a beautiful and revered specimen at the arboretum. *Acer griseum* is a small tree, growing to thirty feet in height, and its stature lends itself to uses in various planting designs, from a single specimen to massing in groves. It can be planted in close proximity to buildings, thus creating intimate interior views to its beautiful bark. Siting paperbark maple in the landscape with a perspective towards the southwest creates a dramatically backlit scenario. The low angle of the winter sun effectively ignites this fiery illusion of peeling bark glowing like curling orange embers.

Combine it with the mounding form and black-green foliage of English spreading yew (*Taxus baccata* 'Repandens') to set off its warm-colored trunks with delightful contrast. I've used it mixed with the copper-colored marcescent foliage of Asian spicebush (*Lindera angustifolia*) above a bronze carpet of *Microbiota decussata* to create a warm and charming winter vignette.

Comprehensively, Japanese maples are endowed with attractive sculptural branching and winter

Acer griseum anchors a vibrant winter vignette.

Acer griseum and *Cornus sanguinea* 'Midwinter Fire' are a winning tonal combination.

armature. Some cultivars are also adorned with vividly colored bark. *Acer palmatum* 'Sango-kaku' is aptly named the coral bark maple. Its coral-red bark is attractive year-round, though its color does become more obvious with leaves shed and more saturated with winter's cold temperatures. This culitvar is a small tree, and like many Japanese maples, it is tolerant of partial shade as well as full sun. Position 'Sango-kaku' where it can easily be seen and enjoyed in the winter garden. I have planted it very close to the house and windows to capitalize on inside winter views. It can be easily trained as a free-standing espalier, forming a red framework of branches in front of glass panes.

The striped or snakebark maples have bark patterns vertically streaked with green and white stripes. This distinctive group includes trees with similar ornamental traits displayed in disjunct species native to North America and Asia.

Acer pensylvanicum is a native to the cold northern woods, a companion to *Betula papyrifera*. It is a small tree, growing in the woodland understory with large, translucent, three-lobed leaves, the largest in the maple family. It ranges from southeastern Canada west to Michigan and through the New England states, south to Pennsylvania, progressing south along the Appalachian peaks to northern Georgia. *Acer pensylvanicum* is known as striped maple, as well as other, more parochial names such as moosewood, goosefoot maple, and whistlewood. The green coloration of the bark is from chloroplasts that photosynthesize even in wintertime, suppyling sustaining sugars long before the broad leaves emerge. The green and white striped bark changes to red in young twigs that are topped with crimson terminal buds. This red anthocyanin pigment is strongly expressed in the rare cultivar 'Erythrocladum'.

Acer palmatum 'Sango-kaku'

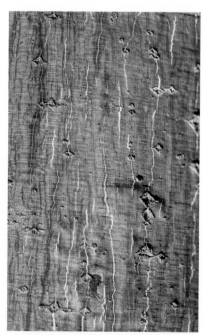

Acer pensylvanicum

Acer pensylvanicum 'Erythrocladum' puts on an unparalleled winter display of coral to salmon-red-colored bark with conspicuous white stripes.

Acer rufinerve

Acer capillipes

Acer tegmentosum

Asian species similar in bark coloration to *Acer pensylvanicum* include *Acer tegmentosum*, the Manchurian striped-bark maple from far-east Russia; *Acer capillipes* and *Acer rufinerve* from Japan; and *Acer davidii* from China. *Acer ×conspicuum* 'Phoenix' is a striking hybrid of two disjunct species, *davidii* and *pensylvanicum*. 'Phoenix' is a small, twenty-foot tree with the most brilliant crimson-red bark with white stripes. The stature and habit of all the striped maple species lend themselves to planting designs for intimate spaces, as well as grouping in groves.

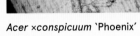

Acer davidii   *Acer ×conspicuum* 'Phoenix'

The primary color yellow is as stimulating as crimson red. Chrome yellow describes the winter essence of *Acer negundo* 'Winter Lightning', a cultivar of the common box elder or ash-leaved maple. It is a medium-size tree native to a broad geographic range throughout continental North America and considered to have little ornamental value. 'Winter Lightning', however, has received the distinguished Award of Garden Merit from the Royal Horticultural Society in England. It responds to pollard pruning with vigorous new stems that turn an intense, brilliant yellow with winter cold. I first observed 'Winter Lightning' at the United States National Arboretum in Washington, D.C., and soon added it to my winter garden palette.

DOGWOOD

Perhaps the most common images of ornamental winter bark are the crimson wands of shrubby dogwoods. Several species of Cornus that are native to the northern latitudes make up this cadre of coppice candidates. *Cornus sericea* is a North American native, while *Cornus sanguinea* is an occupant of European hedgerows, and *Cornus alba* is an Asian equivalent ranging from Siberia to northeast China and Korea. *Cornus alba* 'Westonbirt', also known as 'Sibirica', produces perhaps the most colorful vermillion-red bark. Red twig dogwood (*Cornus sericea*) also sports a yellow-stemmed cultivar called 'Flaviramea'. The coloration of *Cornus sanguinea*

A mass planting of *Cornus sanguinea* 'Midwinter Fire' sets the snow ablaze at Bressingham Gardens in the United Kingdom.

Cornus alba 'Sibirica'

Cornus sericea 'Flaviramea'

Liriope spicata

'Midwinter Fire' lives up to its incendiary name. Its bark has a base pigment of yellow that is overlaid with orange-red hue, which intensifies toward the stems' tips. To make the most impact, combine the colorful stems of any of these cultivars with evergreen foliage. A simple pairing with lilyturf (*Liriope spicata*) creates a satisfying winter scene.

Though shrubby dogwoods are shade tolerant, their pigmentation is most vivid and intense when they're grown in full sun. All of these species of *Cornus* grow as thicket-forming, suckering shrubs and will mature at a height of eight to ten feet. To induce an effective wintry show of colorful stems, they should be grown under suitable cultural conditions and maintained with specific pruning. Their brightly pigmented bark develops on new growth, while the bark on older stems becomes dark and dull. Annual coppice pruning entails cutting the stems back within inches of the ground in early spring. This promotes vigorous new growth with bark that will become brilliantly colored the succeeding winter. These robust new wands can grow four to six feet tall in one season, even after being pruned to the ground. However, the success of this rejuvenation pruning is directly dependant on soil moisture and cultural conditions. *Cornus* species require rich, moisture-retentive soils. If they're planted in light, drought-prone soils and dry conditions, coppice pruning won't result in corresponsive regenerative new growth and colorful bark. In drought conditions, the foliage is also prone to fungal infections, and the bark will become blemished with cankers. These observations are based on my own experience working with the free-draining, sandy loam soils at Tranquil Lake Nursery.

OTHER SPECIES WITH REMARKABLE BARK

Paperbark cherry (*Prunus serrula*) has an outstanding winter presence that is more enduring than its ephemeral springtime flowers. The trunk and branches of paperbark cherry are clothed in glossy, copper-red bark with horizontal encircling bands of lenticels. The bark exfoliates in polished sheets that glow red when backlit by the low angle of the winter sun.

The bark of some trees exfoliates in longitudinal shreds. Shagbark hickory (*Carya ovata*) is the exemplar of this bark pattern. Its trunk is covered in long bark plates that are warped and curled from both ends. Shagbark hickory conveys a unique and easily identifiable winter profile. *Clethra barbinervis, Clethra acuminata, Lagerstroemia* ×'Tuskegee', and *Heptacodium miconioides* also have colorful bark that exfoliates in narrow, vertically oriented shreds and ribbons.

Seven-son flower (*Heptacodium miconioides*) is clothed in light-colored, parchment-beige bark that stands out as an apparition in the landscape. It is a small tree growing to twenty-five feet and can be grown either as a single stem or multi-stemmed tree. It blooms on the current year's growth with fragrant white flowers in September, which allows for heavy spring pruning to both restrict its size and promote flower bud production.

Native to Japan, Korea, and China, kousa dogwood (*Cornus kousa*) is an Asian relative of our indigenous eastern flowering dogwood (*Cornus florida*). Both dogwoods are choice ornamental trees (unlike their shrubby cousins) that bear beautiful bracts, fruit, foliage, and form. The exfoliating, orange-tan mosaic bark of kousa dogwood sets it apart for added winter beauty.

Prunus serrula

Carya ovata

Heptacodium miconioides

Cornus kousa

Parrotia persica

Like kousa dogwood, the bark of Persian iron-wood (*Parrotia persica*) becomes more decorative with age. Its motley appearance can be variable and therefore difficult to describe, much like the blotched patterns of camouflage textiles. However, the visual results are quite the opposite: Its coloration does not disguise and obscure its trunk, but brings it into attention-getting focus.

Lacebark pine (*Pinus bungeana*) is unique among conifers. It appears like the mythical chimera, composed of parts from dissimilar creatures. A native of

Pinus bungeana

Stewartia pseudocamellia

Salix alba 'Britzensis' coppiced to force sprouts

OPPOSITE Ledge-cropped and boulder-strewn barrens in Downeast Maine are home to hundreds of acres of lowbush blueberry (*Vaccinium angustifolium*).

China, this pine sports the mottled trunk and branches associated with a sycamore. Lacebark pine is a most strikingly beautiful specimen when grown with multiple, low-branched trunks. The bark flakes off in an irregular patchwork of caulk white, yellow, tan, and gray-green. London plane tree (*Platanus ×acerifolia*) has bark that exfoliates in similar patterns and colors. 'Suttneri' is an albino cultivar of London plane tree sheathed in chalk white.

If I were to choose one genera of tree with the best mottled bark, *Stewartia* would be my choice. A superlative specimen of *Stewartia pseudocamellia* raised from seed collected by E. H. Wilson in 1917 in South Korea is a prominent part of the Arnold Arboretum's collection in Boston. Though not as venerable, the Polly Hill Arboretum on Martha's Vineyard holds an outstanding collection of several *Stewartia* species.

Stewartia pseudocamellia has ornamental stature year-round. It blooms with white camellia-like flowers in early summer, and its foliage turns to a blaze of orange in autumn. Its bark is both sensual and alluring, satin smooth and mottled in shades of salmon-orange, tan, and beige. This colorful bark is the sustaining feature that gives *Stewartia* prominence in the winter garden. It's a medium-size tree with upright branching, a form that facilitates fairly snug spacing, whether situated in groves of multiple trees or close to structures.

Like the shrubby dogwoods, various willow species are associated with the coppice pruning technique. This method is used to produce crops of flexible willow stems for wickerwork and basketry. White willow (*Salix alba*) grows into a large tree, but when coppiced to the ground, its stump sprouts wondrous wands. 'Britzensis' and 'Chermesina' are two forms that have brightly colored winter bark. *Salix* ×'Scarlet Curls' is a weeping form of willow with twisted and contoured red-tinged branches.

The woody stems of Japanese kerria (*Kerria japonica*) are clothed in apple-green bark, a color that seems to defy the winter season. Japanese kerria is a suckering shrub growing to six feet in height. Its form is fine-textured, a multitude of vertical green linearity. This old-fashioned summer-blooming shrub can still set a striking pose in winter snow.

Oakleaf hydrangea (*Hydrangea quercifolia*) is the aristocrat of the hydrangea family. It reigns with year-round presence in the garden, often celebrated in the shady border for its large, conical heads of white sterile flowers and strongly lobed leaves. Its foliage turns red to purple in autumn, but in winter, its exfoliating bark takes the stage. I like to pair *Hydrangea quercifolia* with the glossy, pinnately compound evergreen foliage of leatherleaf mahonia (*Mahonia bealei*).

Lowbush blueberry (*Vaccinium angustifolium*) forms a low groundcover of reddish, finely branched stems topped with fat red terminal buds. A color gradient of genetic diversity, or *grex*, it features stems ranging in color from deep red to pink and pale green, making a dappled mosaic. Lowbush blueberry is a valuable, drought-tolerant addition to an array of plants with colorful bark for the winter garden—and a favorite fruit for summer pies. Much like the bark of deciduous trees and shrubs as a design feature in the garden, its form belies the magnitude of its ornamental stature in the winter landscape.

PART II
SIGNS
OF
LIFE

Chapter Five

Emergent
Flower Buds

Subtle signs of winter life are like rare jewels whose charm should not be overlooked. In the winter garden, these rarefied details may often be found in the structures that enclose and protect future blooms. Many trees and shrubs produce flower buds that are in fact on display all winter long. Some winter buds have a quiet beauty, while others are as highly decorative as their full flowers will be when in bloom.

Unlike the foliage and flower buds of herbaceous plants that take shape as plants emerge in a flush of new growth, some woody shrubs make their flower buds and enclosed blossoms on the new growth of the current season's woody stems. Panicled hydrangea (*Hydrangea paniculata* cvs.) is an example. Others, such as common lilac (*Syringa vulgaris*), form flower buds toward the end of summer on mature growth. These flower buds endure the winter season and open the following spring. The most valuable plants for the winter garden will produce an array of persistent flower buds that display exceptional ornamental qualities throughout that season. It is

Magnolia ×kewensis 'Wada's Memory'

noteworthy that their decorative presentation may last for six months, whereas most flowers themselves only last for a fleeting few weeks.

Skimmia japonica is a shade-loving broadleaf evergreen shrub with a spreading form that grows to a height of three feet. This Asian native belongs to the citrus family (Rutaceae) and is hardy to Zone 6. Japanese skimmia is dioecious, with male and female flowers developing on separate individual plants. It blooms in April, and the pollinated female flower forms clusters of shiny red fruit that ripen in fall and persist all winter. Male Japanese skimmia is distinct among dioecious plants and has a peculiar avian quality, whereby the male is typically showier than the female. The male plant's flower buds, displayed on large, rounded terminal panicles, create a striking rose-colored show—larger and more colorful than the female's small, pale buds. Japanese skimmia's prominent winter display of panicled male flower buds rivals its red fruit (which comes later) in ornamental beauty.

The eye-catching winter flower buds of edgeworthia (*Edgeworthia chrysantha*) are curious and exotic, hanging pendulously from the branch tips like silken silver purses. They are shaped like round squat bundles with a bulging form, suggesting a compressed umbelliferous cluster of tubular buds. This edgeworthia species

Skimmia japonica

Edgeworthia chrysantha

Corylus fargesii catkins

is referenced to Zone 7, and it flourishes at the Scott Arboretum in Swarthmore, Pennsylvania. However, edgeworthia has also been thriving for five years at the former Allen C. Haskell Nursery in New Bedford, Massachusetts, which is now preserved as a public garden.

A catkin is a distinct flower structure found on birches, willows, alders, and filberts. It looks like a tightly plaited cord and consists of a long, cylindrically compacted cluster of apetalous flowers. By its definition, a catkin does not have covering bud scales or petals. It does, however, have an ornamental winter charm.

Farges filbert (*Corylus fargesii*) is represented in the collections of the Morris Arboretum and Gardens

of the University of Pennsylvania and Arnold Arboretum of Harvard University in Boston. These trees were grown from seed collected on a 1996 collaborative expedition to Shaanxi and Gansu, China. It is a medium-size tree with exquisite, exfoliating cream and copper-colored bark. The winter branches of Farges filbert are festooned with pendulous clusters of copper-colored tassels. Though still relatively rare, this tree was honored by the International Dendrology Society as Tree of the Year in 2016. It can withstand Zone 5 temperatures.

The winter buds of some magnolias actually resemble the fuzzy catkins of pussy willow. Star magnolia (*Magnolia stellata*), *Magnolia* ×*kewensis* 'Wada's

Magnolia stellata

Memory', and *Magnolia ×soulangeana* 'Cadolleana' all have large winter flower buds densely coated in silver gray hairs, lustrous filaments that gleam in winter sun.

The obvious winter feature common to mountain andromeda (*Pieris floribunda*), Japanese andromeda (*P. japonica*), and their interspecific hybrid cross 'Brouwer's Beauty' andromeda (*P. ×*'Brouwer's Beauty') is their glossy broadleaf evergreen foliage. However, their showy flower buds are outstanding winter trimmings. Andromedas' characteristic inflorescence structure is a branched panicle of racemes, and variation in these inflorescences' geometry is key to distinguishing one from another: Mountain andromeda features an upright pattern of buds, while the Japanese species is pendulous, and their hybrid progeny display a horizontal form.

Japanese andromeda's dangling strands of flower buds fall over its cloak of green foliage like braided epaulets, ivory colored and strung on pale, light-red peduncles and pedicels. The vibrant buds of *Pieris japonica* 'Dorothy Wycoff' bring a jeweled display to its glossy green leaves. The entire branched panicle is crimson and studded with scarlet buds, arrayed like pendants set with pear-cut rubies. The buds of *Pieris ×*'Brouwer's Beauty', on the other hand, are salmon pink. When grown in full sun, these tufts become a vivid henna color in winter.

Pale ivory-colored flower buds embellish the winter display of mountain andromeda (*Pieris floribunda*). These are arranged on vertically forked panicles and open in early spring into white urn-shaped flowers. The sprightly, upright form of mountain andromeda's inflorescence gives it a unique charm.

Pieris japonica

Pieris japonica `Dorothy Wycoff`

Pieris ×`Brouwer's Beauty`

Pieris floribunda

Pieris japonica
var. *yakushimensis*
'Cavatine'

Cornus florida

Pieris floribunda has become scarce in the contemporary horticulture market. This beautiful evergreen shrub is native to the high elevations of the southern Appalachian Mountains. Although *Pieris floribunda* grows well in field-grown nursery production, it has finicky requirements that don't fit into the standard conventions of container plant production.

Pieris japonica var. *yakushimensis* 'Cavatine' flower buds are upright panicled racemes. Although a meager stand-in for *Pieris floribunda*, it is a beautiful dwarf Japanese andromeda. The winter flower buds of 'Cavatine' are ivory with pale pink overlay and pink penduncles and pedicels.

Last but not least, dogwood (*Cornus florida*) branches must be mentioned, as they're distinguished in the winter landscape by their terminal mitered buds. Four clasping, chalk-white bracts form these botanical turbans. The subtle detail of dogwood this time of year is key to comprehending the beauty of the winter garden.

Chapter Six

Winter-Blooming Trees and Shrubs

Flowers are emblematic representations of life. When serendipitous blossoms appear in a season seemingly devoid of life, they produce one of the most joyful aspects of the winter gardening season. And a diverse array of plants displays showy flowers during the cold of winter. Extraordinarily, this marvel occurs even here in Massachusetts.

WITCH HAZEL

Unlike blossoms in other seasons, the winter bloom sequence is somewhat unpredictable and doesn't adhere to a strict schedule of dates. Even if erratic weather causes winter's phenologic timing to be uncertain, witch hazels are dependable florescent bookends to the winter bloom season. Native witch hazel (*Hamamelis virginiana*) marks the beginning with a flourish of yellow flowers in November. Its quill-like flowers make a show after its leaves have dropped. They are made up of yellow strap-shaped petals arranged in starry clusters along the branches. In sheltered garden settings, native witch hazel flowers can continue their show through December.

Chinese witch hazel (*Hamamelis mollis*) and Asian hybrid cultivars such as 'Arnold Promise' (*Hamamelis ×intermedia* 'Arnold Promise') provide the winter floral finale in March. I find the sweet fragrance of *Hamamelis mollis* 'Wisley Supreme' to be the most potent and enjoyable. The scent of its pale-yellow flowers can be detected from a distance. Other hybrid cultivars to consider include 'Ostergold', 'Danny', and 'Aurora'.

Witch hazels can be found in a diversity of shapes, branching habits, and heights. While size is variable, some can grow to the size of a small tree, attaining a height of twenty-five feet or more. Some cultivars have a vase-shaped profile, while others spread more, with horizontal form. Witch hazels perform well in partial shade under a high tree canopy or in full sun. Flower bud development is most bountiful when they're grown in a sunny position with moisture-retentive soil.

Witch hazel cultivars are propagated by grafting, usually on an understock of common witch hazel

(*Hamamelis virginiana*) or Persian ironwood (*Parrotia persica*). Care should be given to monitoring the understock union for any unwanted sucker growth. Suckers will appear below the graft union; they are part of the understock, not the desired cultivar. Unchecked understock development turns a choice plant into an unsightly mongrel with dissimilar flowers and forms. Top grafting on a high, straight understock of *Parrotia* produces a splendid, standard-form witch hazel tree. This configuration allows for a tiered planting design. A layer of the coarse-textured, evergreen foliage of leatherleaf mahonia (*Mahonia bealei*) planted beneath the witch hazels creates quite a display.

Witch hazel flowers last for many weeks. They are particularly well adapted to withstanding winter weather. Reacting like a thermostatic gauge, the petals curl up into tight bundles in response to extremely cold temperatures and unfurl once again when the mercury rises. This novel adaptation protects the flowers, and their showy display, from the ravages of inclement weather.

BELOW *Hamamelis virginiana*
BOTTOM *Hamamelis ×intermedia 'Arnold Promise'*

ABOVE *Hamamelis mollis* 'Wisley Supreme'
OPPOSITE *Hamamelis virginiana* 'Harvest Moon'

*Hamamelis
×intermedia*
'Ostergold'

*Hamamelis
×intermedia*
'Danny'

*Hamamelis
×intermedia*
'Jelena'

*Hamamelis
×intermedia*
'Aurora'

The chroma of witch hazel flowers is decidedly on the warm side, generally spanning the color spectrum between yellow and red. These subtle hues are beautifully and categorically described in the book *Witch Hazels* by Chris Lane as citron, lemon yellow, pale yellow, sulfur yellow, burnt orange, copper orange, light orange, carmine red, and claret red. Their pigmentation offers a welcome warmth in contrast to winter snow.

'Jelena' blooms early to midwinter, some years appearing before Christmas. I designed a garden using several top-grafted tree form 'Jelena' planted in a row to form a frieze of trained branches in front of a band of windows. The winter view through these windows from inside is a showstopper, and the bright winter flowers contribute to the warmth of the room.

Vernal witch hazel (*Hamamelis vernalis*) is usually the first to bloom, starting in early January. It has a spicy fragrance. Worthy cultivars include yellow 'Sandra' and aptly named 'Red Imp'. The cultivar 'Amethyst' displays flowers that are an alluring shade of violet.

My list of favorite witch hazels is growing all the time. I am also very fond of a Japanese selection named *Hamamelis japonica* 'Shibamichi Red'. It sports uniquely colored cerise flowers that are also mildly fragrant.

The breadth of the witch hazel collection at The Polly Hill Arboretum on Martha's Vineyard is superb. A winter visit prompted me to acquire *Hamamelis ×intermedia* 'Ostergold'. The Scott Arboretum in Swarthmore, Pennsylvania also has a comprehensive collection of witch hazels planted throughout its grounds. They are integrated into an inspiringly designed landscape with many other plants to complement the winter garden.

Hamamelis ×intermedia 'Jelena', a graft on Parrotia to create an upright tree form. Their copper orange flowers are my all-time favorite.

'Sandra' (above left) and 'Red Imp' (above right) are cultivars of vernal witch hazel (*Hamamelis vernalis*).

Hamamelis japonica 'Shibamichi Red'

Mahonia bealei

Combine mahonia's fervent form and flowers with the muted elegance of the copper-colored foliage held by Asian spicebush (*Lindera angustifolia*) for a winter garden spectacle.

Mahonia ×media 'Charity'

MAHONIA

The idea of a warm winter day may be cold comfort; however, some plants need only the slightest warmth to nudge their flower buds into bloom. Mahonia is an upright evergreen shrub clothed in sharp, pinnately compound leaves. The radial arrangement of its glossy green foliage exaggerates its coarse texture. This impressive foliar composition is topped off with a terminal inflorescence of yellow fireworks. A dusting of white snow amplifies the winter display.

Leatherleaf mahonia (*Mahonia bealei*) is a particularly precocious flowering shrub. Its urn-shaped yellow flowers are arranged in tight clusters along upright compound racemes. These fragrant flowers frequently open in early winter, even in December. Although full bloom is often interrupted by winter's cold, the waxy buds and flowers are quite enduring and will resume opening when agreeable weather returns.

I've grown *Mahonia bealei* in sheltered niches in Zone 5 gardens. However, *Mahonia ×media* 'Charity', the hybrid of *Mahonia japonica* and *Mahonia lomariifolia*, is hardy only to Zone 7. It sports stunning erect racemes of flowers and oversized, tropical whorls of pinnately compound leaves. It flourishes in an exuberant garden in Little Compton, Rhode Island.

CHERRY

Celebrating the advent of cherry blossom season is a long-practiced tradition with historical origins linked to Japan. The bright spring flowers of cherry represent the philosophical embodiment of both beauty and mortality, signifying life and rebirth at the commencement of the growing season. The fragile, ephemeral nature of their petals exemplifies life's conclusion.

The seasonal duality of the winter-blooming cherry (*Prunus ×subhirtella* 'Autumnalis') brings both characterizations together. This hardy small tree celebrates both spring and winter with clouds of delicate pale pink flowers gracing its branches. 'Autumnalis' cherry adorns the entrance to historic Swan Point Cemetery in Providence, Rhode Island. This cultivar of Higan cherry is quite reliable in its precociousness. In mid-December, the flower-bud scales dehisce and unfurl into a pink petaled spectacle. Snow adds an extra layer of wonder to this phenomenal horticultural celebration. And as if by magic, these cherries flourish once more in the spring. It is an amazing encore of additional pink-petaled blooms.

Prunus mume, the Japanese apricot, has also been celebrated for its colorful winter bloom. This small tree is native to China and Korea, where it has been cultivated for millennia. Its fragrant, clove-scented flowers are a sensual winter garden treat in January. It is much less hardy than its flowering cherry relatives and rarely found in gardens north of New York City. I have appreciated seeing and smelling Japanese apricot's bright blooms against drifts of snow at the Scott Arboretum in Swarthmore, Pennsylvania in January and February. The cultivar 'Matsubara Red' has double, deep rose flowers. *Prunus mume* 'Kobai' blooms with semi-double pink flowers.

Prunus ×subhirtella `Autumnalis'

Prunus mume `Kobai'

Prunus mume `Matsubara Red'

CAMELLIA

Camellias are the most exotic and enchanting of winter flowers. The ruffled winter petals form luxurious flowers as exquisite as roses. These evergreen shrubs, native to China and Japan, were introduced to western horticulture in the eighteenth century. Once, they were grown only in glasshouses or in southern gardens from Virginia to the Gulf Coast. Thanks to Dr. William Ackerman's breakthrough breeding program with *Camellia oleifera* at the US National Arboretum, accompanied by Dr. Clifford Parks at the University of North Carolina, cultivars of new camellias are winter hardy to Zone 6. These hardy camellia hybrids are a welcome addition to select micro-climates in coastal southern New England and Long Island, New York gardens. Camellias thrive best when planted in a niche protected from desiccating winter wind and sun. Plant a hardy, winter-blooming camellia, shaded by the canopy of *Prunus ×subhirtella* 'Autumnalis' or *Prunus mume*. This will make a great beginning to a spectacular winter garden.

I have Dr. Ackerman's cultivar *Camellia* ×'Winter's Snowman' thriving in a Cape Cod garden sheltered by the lee of the house and shaded by an evergreen sweet bay magnolia (*Magnolia virginiana* 'Henry Hicks'). It is planted with an evergreen skirt of sweetbox (*Sarcococca hookeriana* var. *humilis*). The semi-double white flowers of 'Winter's Snowman' bloom in December. November and December-blooming cultivars of hardy camellias are more reliable in the northeast than hybrids that bloom in late winter and early spring.

Camellia blooms range from single-petaled flowers centered with a boss of yellow stamens to double and semi-double forms. *Camellia* ×'Autumn Spirit' is a double rose-pink gem bred by Dr. Parks. It blooms in December along with Dr. Ackerman's *Camellia* ×'Ashton's Ballet'. Dr. Takayuki Tanaka's introduction, *Camellia* ×vernalis 'Mieko Tanaka', is a riveting single-petalled, red-centered flower with bright yellow stamens. The vermillion blooms are complemented by dark, glossy green foliage.

Pair the late-November-blooming native witch hazel (*Hamamelis virginiana*) with *Camellia* ×'Long Island Pink' for a dramatic "opposites attract" effect in the winter garden. Austere, quill-like petals of witch hazel are striking in contrast to the voluptuous, full, pink-petaled flowers. And witch hazel's flowers mimic the camellia's projecting yellow stamens. The copper-colored foliage of Asian spicebush (*Lindera angustifolia*) is also a beautiful foil to the rose-toned camellia flowers and their glossy evergreen leaves.

Salix gracilistyla

Salix myrsinifolia, also known as *Salix nigricans*

Salix chaenomeloides

Salix gracilistyla 'Mount Aso'

WILLOW

Winter blooms range from the seemingly exotic to the familiar and comforting. Fuzzy pussy willows blossom in late winter. Their well-known silver white catkins covered in silky hairs are quite an oddity, botanically speaking. These furry pelt-like flowers have a unique anatomy that resembles an animal rather than a plant. Willow's pubescent catkins are actually elongated wads comprised of many flowers compressed together and containing no sepals or petals. The fuzzy, vertical spikes are arranged in close order along the stems. Willows are dioecious, with male and female flowers on different plants.

American pussy willow (*Salix discolor*) blooms in March. It is indigenous to swampy environments throughout the northeastern United States and Canada. Many large willows respond positively to hard spring pruning, sprouting vigorous new wands that will be adorned with blooms the following winter.

The rose-gold pussy willow (*Salix gracilistyla*) is native to China, Japan, and Korea. The young male flowers are covered with gray silk, through which reddish, unopened anthers can be seen. As the male flowers mature, their anthers become bright yellow to orange. As they are laden with pollen, the effect is like a miniature explosion of shooting fireworks.

Willows can also be attractive to pollinators as they search for food on warm winter days. The dark-leaved willow (*Salix myrsinifolia*, also called *Salix nigricans*) has striking black stems covered with white pubescence. It is native to northern England and Scotland. Japanese pussy willow (*Salix chaenomeloides*) is found in Korea and China, as well as Japan. It grows into a large, vigorous shrub that comes into bloom in

January. *Salix gracilistyla* 'Mount Aso' blooms with alluringly rose-pink catkins.

OTHER WINTER-FLOWERING SPECIES

JASMINE

Winter jasmine (*Jasminum nudiflorum*) blooms with bright yellow star-shaped flowers on bare green branches. It has a recumbent habit of growth, and its green stems spread over banks and cascade over walls. Its winter bloom time is variable, subject to the weather, but brightens the garden regardless. Here, it has flowered as early as mid-January and as late as the first of March. It is especially beautiful combined with the gold foliage of *Ilex crenata* 'Drops of Gold' or the gold-variegated leaves of *Acuba japonica* 'Variegata'.

WINTERSWEET

The Chinese wintersweet (*Chimonanthus praecox* 'Luteus') is spectacular in the late-winter garden. This eight-foot-tall deciduous shrub blooms with pendant, waxy, translucent yellow bells that wreath its branches. Dusted with snow, its dangling inflorescence glows. The pale yellow flowers are very fragrant, exuding a spicy and exotic scent. It is hardy in Zone 7, and with protection in Zone 6, though I have not seen *Chimonanthus* grown north of New York Botanical Gardens in the Bronx.

DAPHNE

Daphne ×transatlantica 'Eternal Fragrance' has a wide-ranging bloom season. In Massachusetts,

Jasminum nudiflorum

Chimonanthus praecox

Daphne xtransatlantica 'Eternal Fragrance'

the fragrant flowers open with a flourish in May. It then continues to bloom intermittently throughout the summer, with a spate of intensified flowering in autumn that often extends into November and early winter.

The paperbush (*Edgeworthia chrysantha*), or simply edgeworthia, is an impressive member of the daphne family that is a showstopper in the winter garden, blooming with sweet gardenia-scented flowers. This six-foot rounded deciduous shrub is native to woodland areas in the Himalayas and China and is hardy to Zone 7. In winter, exotically decorative, silvery flower

Edgeworthia chrysantha

buds top the branch tips. At the Scott Arboretum in Swarthmore, Pennsylvania, *Edgeworthia chrysantha* begins to bloom around the end of February. The fat, lustrous buds expand to flower heads composed of an umbelliferous cluster of up to forty nodding, tubular flowers. Their silky white sheath opens up to a burst of brilliant yellow. Though it's not hardy in much of New England, a friend and keen horticulturist reports that edgeworthia is thriving in her Plymouth, Massachusetts garden.

HONEYSUCKLE

The sense of smell arouses the strongest memories, and the sweet fragrance of winter honeysuckle (*Lonicera fragrantissima*) takes me back in time and place to January 1991 with horticulturist friends at the Morris Arboretum and Gardens of the University of Pennsylvania, where I first met this fragrant winter bloomer. It is a large shrub with semi-persistent foliage and flowers that open throughout the winter on the warmest days.

DOGWOOD

The bright yellow flowers of the cornelian cherry dogwood (*Cornus mas*) signal the waning of winter. It is a reliable March bloomer in southern New England. The fat, turban-shaped flower buds are enclosed by four bracts, which open into a showy burst of bright yellow blooms arranged in umbel clusters of petaloid bracts. Cornelian cherry dogwood grows to be a small tree, often in a multi-trunked form. It is hardy to Zone 4, and its radiant blooms were a welcome turning point in the winter weather when I was a horticulture student at the University of Maine in Orono. Native to Europe and western Asia, it will grow in partial shade to full sun.

There are several named cultivars of cornelian cherry dogwood. *Cornus mas* 'Spring Glow' is a

Lonicera fragrantissima

Cornus mas 'Spring Glow'

J. C. Raulston introduction from the eponymous North Carolina State University Arboretum. It is considered one of the best cultivars for gardens in the southern United States. Blooming at the end of February at the Scott Arboretum of Swarthmore College in Pennsylvania is a sizeable specimen of 'Spring Glow'. It has a commanding presence with its broad branches, spreading greater than its height.

The Japanese cornel dogwood (*Cornus officinalis*) is an Asian relative that is very similar to *Cornus mas*, though it is native to China, Japan, and Korea, and hardy to Zone 5. *Cornus officinalis* 'Lemon Zest' is an introduction from the Morris Arboretum and Gardens of the University of Pennsylvania in Philadelphia. It has lemon-scented bright yellow flowers that are displayed on longer-than-normal pedicels, making it showier than the species. *Cornus officinalis* 'Kintoki' is another cultivar, introduced to the United States by Barry Yinger through Brookside Gardens in Wheaton, Maryland.

Cornus officinalis 'Lemon Zest'

Erica carnea 'Springwood White'

HEATH AND HEATHER

Winter heath (*Erica carnea*) is a sub-shrub with fine-textured, evergreen needle-like leaves. It blooms in late winter and early spring. The dainty bell-like flowers tend to first open during January thaws and continue to bloom on mild winter days in late February and March. *Erica carnea* 'December Red', Springwood White, 'Springwood Pink', 'Winter Beauty', and *Erica ×darleyensis* 'Mary Helen' and 'Silberschmelze' are a few common cultivars of heath. Their flowers, though tiny, are profuse. In bloom, the entire plant is transformed into hummocks of pink or white.

Heaths and heathers (*Calluna*) are native to Europe and often connected to the wild flora found on the moors of Scotland. My fond association with heath is tied to a garden on the coast of Maine. Beatrix Farrand's Ericaceae collection from her Reef Point Gardens in Bar Harbor was transplanted to create the Asticou Azalea Garden in Northeast Harbor. It was in this Japanese-style stroll garden where I was first charmed by this lilliputian shrub.

The best cultural conditions for winter heath are full sun and organically rich, free-draining soil. It is best planted in masses and is a pleasing textural companion to very dwarf conifers.

Erica carnea at the Asticou Azalea Garden, Maine

MAPLE

Winter's close is heralded by the flowering of a tree known more for its autumn foliage. The scarlet blooms of the red maple tree (*Acer rubrum*) are a harbinger of the emergent flush of spring. Red maple has an extensive native geographical range from Canada south to Florida. The diminutive size of its red flowers, displayed on red pedicels, is compensated for by their sheer quantity. Together, they emblazon the landscape with a vibrant crimson haze. Red maple phenology blazes a colorful trail across its range; its blooms are a beautiful record of the season's progression from winter to spring.

Many cultivars of *Acer rubrum* have been selected for their brilliant fall foliage color as well as their distinctive habit of growth. *Acer rubrum* 'Weepy' is a rare form, selected by horticulturist L. Clarence Towe, with pendulous branches and a smaller stature than

Acer rubrum

the species. 'Weepy' red maple grows to become a sculptural, rounded mound, forming a tree that is as broad as it is high.

Rarer though they may be, colorful blooms offer a magical delight to the garden. More than in any other season, in winter, flowers are especially savored.

Chapter Seven

Winter Fruits

Fruits or fruit-like plant structures can make colorful contributions to the winter garden. Many woody plants notable for fruit are monoecious, meaning individual plants' flowers include both male (stamen) and female (pistil) parts. Thus they are self-fertile, though these plants often benefit from cross-pollination and planting in multiples. Others are dioecious, with male and female flowers produced on separate, distinct plants.

Several dioecious plants happen to share an ecological niche in addition to this reproductive characteristic, including salt shrub, bayberry, and winterberry holly. In combination, they can be used to create coastal habitat-inspired winter scenes.

The frothy white seedheads of salt shrub (*Baccharis halimifolia*) are showier than its blooms. This woody member of the aster family, Asteraceae, is found in brackish coastal estuaries from Maine to Texas. The briny, wet habitat belies its terrestrial ability and tolerance of dry, drought-prone soils. *Baccharis* can grow to ten feet tall; however, because it blooms on new growth, early hard pruning can control its size to four feet without impeding late fall flowering. Female plants put on an extra show: The seedheads are covered with a silver-white feathery pappus, or modified calyx, that resembles small brushes with long white bristles. I have planted *Baccharis* with Arkansas bluestar (*Amsonia hubrichtii*) in an unirrigated, sunny garden placed next to the scorching heat of an asphalt driveway. The duo put on a spectacle in mid-November. These white tasseled seedheads coincide with early winter blooms of native witch hazel (*Hamamelis virginiana*), red fruit of winterberry holly, and the blues of bayberry.

Bayberry (*Morella pensylvanica*, formerly *Myrica pensylvanica*) is an exceedingly tough, drought- and salt-tolerant shrub for full sun. It is hardy to Zone 2. Apart from its rugged qualities, its leaves and the blue berries are delightfully aromatic. They render a wax utilized in fragrant bayberry candles. It is also dioecious and requires a male flowering plant to pollinate a fruit bearing female plant. Bayberry is often propagated from seed, and this produces plant seedlings that are a mix of sexes. Very few nurseries select

Baccharis halimifolia (above and right)

Ilex verticillata

Myrica pensylvanica (above and right)

and separate female and male plants or propagate bayberry from vegetative cuttings made from female stock plants. When choosing from unsexed plants at a nursery, finding remnant fruit is one means to identify a female plant. The Morton Arboretum west of Chicago has selected and trademarked a female clone of bayberry and named it 'Silver Sprite'. This cultivar is not superior to any other female bayberry, other than that it is commercially labeled and verified to be a female clone.

Winterberry holly (*Ilex verticillata*) is a deciduous shrub and grows throughout an extensive native geographic range from wet woods and swamps in Newfoundland, Quebec, and Ontario in Canada, wild landscapes through New England, south down the Atlantic seaboard to Florida, west to Mississippi, and north to the Great Lakes region. This wide-ranging habitat and its hardiness account for the winterberry holly's immense popularity among gardeners, horticulturists, and environmentalists.

Winterberry holly can be found growing in many diverse environmental niches, from shady, wet thicket to sunny seaside exposure buffeted by salt-laden winds. (The stunning wild specimen pictured here is growing in a wave-compiled seawall moraine on the coast of the Schoodic Peninsula in Maine.) Drought-stressed plants will not develop abundant flower buds, and these hollies do prefer a planting location with moisture-retentive soils and full sun. This environment is most conducive for flower formation and subsequent fruit.

Like all hollies, winterberry is dioecious. It requires the planting of a male pollinator for the fruiting female. Because bees are industrious searchers for flowers, male holly is an effective pollinator even when it is not

Ilex verticillata

planted adjacent to a female plant, and sometimes as far away as a half mile. In Massachusetts, winterberry holly blooms on new growth in late June. The fruits mature in clusters along the stems and reach their full coloration in September, set against green foliage. The real attention-getting show begins after leaf drop in late November.

Geography and phenology are explicitly interrelated and consequential in selecting the gender of cultivars for pollination of *Ilex verticillata*. An individual male holly's flowers from a northern population will not bloom in coordination with a female derived from a southern clone. Such a mismatch of geographical genders will result in no pollination and no fruit production. I have experienced this regional bloom incomparability within wild winterberry holly populations, even between New England states. I once planted a large fruited female cultivar named 'Jolly Red' in Maine. It had been selected from a wild Connecticut population of winterberry holly by Bloomfield, Connecticut nurseryman Ludwig Hoffman. To my amazement, the bloom time of the local Maine males didn't coincide with the transplant. Two male cultivars that are common in the nursery trade are 'Southern Gentleman' and 'Jim Dandy', but check with your local horticulturists for regional cultivar pollination data.

The fruit color of winterberry holly ranges from shades of red to orange and yellow. Yellow-fruited *Ilex verticillata* f. 'Chrysocarpa' was collected in the wild in Massachusetts around 1900. Deeper yellow 'Winter Gold' is an introduction from Simpson Nursery in Indiana. The most dwarf form of winterberry holly, 'Red Sprite', has exceptionally large fruit displayed on a compact, four-foot-tall shrub.

The bare-branched display of winterberry holly's red fruit—like the fruit of *Baccharis*—nicely coincides with the yellow blooms of native witch hazel (*Hamamelis virginiana*) in November. Winterberry holly is very effective in large borders or hedgerows

Ilex verticillata f. 'Chrysocarpa' (opposite and above)

Ilex verticillata 'Winter Gold'

Ilex verticillata 'Red Sprite'

with red twig dogwood, or as a specimen highlighting a small garden. Place it next to walkways and directly in view outside of windows to capitalize on the winter enjoyment it brings.

Many evergreen holly species also have ornamental winter fruit. American holly (*Ilex opaca*) and others are discussed in a chapter on broadleaf evergreens, with the one exception of *Ilex glabra* f. 'Leucocarpa', the white-fruited form of inkberry holly. Its stark white fruit displayed against evergreen leaves stands out in a species of holly normally known for black fruit.

Moving on from the coast-inspired trio of salt bush, bayberry, and winterberry holly, summertime flowers yield colorful fruits from monoecious and dioecious plants. Many persist and make valuable contributions to a decorative wintertime show. Indeed, the

Ilex glabra 'Leucocarpa'

scope of trees and shrubs with ornamental fruit for use in winter gardens in Massachusetts is vast. They encompass tree forms such as crabapple and procumbent ground huggers like cranberry. The diversity includes the exotic globes of hardy orange and the familiar red hairy drupes of sumac. Some fruits are colorful enough to earn their place, even if only for a brief time in late fall and early winter, though their brilliance is tarnished after a hard freeze. This is the case for the violet orbs of 'Early Amethyst' beautyberry (*Callicarpa dichotoma* 'Early Amethyst'), as well as the white-fruited 'Leucocarpa' beautyberry (*C. japonica* 'Leucocarpa'). They only hold their winter garden value through December.

Growing plants as a food source for pollinators and birds is a primary principle for cultivating an environmentally friendly and beautiful garden. However, winter fruit displays can disappear quickly, not from freezing weather, but from hungry birds gobbling them up too soon. The scarlet-red fruit of winterberry holly often doesn't last through December, but some ornamental fruits are spared such hungry ravages. Those of 'Brilliantissima' red chokeberry (*Aronia arbutifolia*), a cultivar of a native plant, are not particularly palatable to wildlife, thus they persist as ornamental elements in the winter garden. Red chokeberry is an upright-growing deciduous shrub that has great garden versatility both culturally and visually. It is often found in the wild growing on the wooded edge of a moist meadow. It is actually highly drought tolerant, thriving in dry conditions in either full sun or partial shade. The upright growth form of 'Brilliantissima' provides for easy integration into a mixed herbaceous border with perennials mingling around its base. It can also be used to make a fairly narrow hedge. Clusters of

Callicarpa dichotoma 'Early Amethyst'

Callicarpa japonica 'Leucocarpa'

Aronia arbutifolia 'Brilliantissima'

white flowers bloom in May and mature into red fruits, which ripen in September. These accompany blazing red fall foliage in October. The fruits are long-lasting and add welcome color to the winter garden.

Nandina domestica 'Royal Princess' is an upright-growing shrub with tripinnately compound evergreen leaves. Its finely textured, bamboo-like foliage is the origin of its common name, heavenly bamboo; it is actually a member of the Berberidaceae family. Nandina blooms with small white flowers arranged in a long terminal raceme, and this flower structure transforms into a dense cluster of bright red berries. The foliage is semi-evergreen in southern New England and acquires an orange cast in the fall. Though this native of China and Japan is hardy to Zone 6, it doesn't bloom well in New England and consequently does not put on the heavy winter show of red fruit like that seen in the Philadelphia region.

I love sumac! This highly ornamental native deserves much adoration. Sadly, the genus *Rhus* has often been misunderstood by the general public—even the mention of its name connotes an association with

poison. The red fruits of staghorn sumac (*Rhus typhina*) are, in fact, a very edible, lemony 'spice' known to creative cooks. Its native range is almost as extensive as winterberry holly, throughout eastern Canada and the United States, south to Georgia and west to Iowa. It is hardy from Zone 3 to 8. Sumac's flower, like holly's, is dioecious, and its flowers are an important nectar source for bees. I am particularly fond of the female cut-leaf clone of staghorn sumac *Rhus typhina* 'Laciniata'. It grows from a suckering shrub to a small tree clothed in lacy, bipinnately compound leaves that turn fiery shades of orange and red in fall. The greenish female flowers of 'Laciniata' transform into pyramidally shaped fuzzy clusters of scarlet-red fruit that are displayed on stout pubescent stems.

Rhus typhina 'Laciniata'

If sumac is to be described as ubiquitous and commonplace, then hardy orange (*Poncirus trifoliata*) is certainly the opposite. This distinct citrus from northern China is hardy to Zone 6. It grows to be a large shrub or a small tree made up of green stems barbed with the most menacing thorns. It casts a singular profile. The fruits are miniature oranges, intriguingly ornamental but inedible.

The collections of flowering crabapples, which constitute significant portions of many arboreta and botanic gardens, demonstrate their ornamental value in temperate gardens. Their fragrant flowers are certainly a delight in May. Crabapples are trees to be grown in full sun and are generally hardy to Zone 4. Their form and size vary greatly, from upright to spreading to pendantly weeping. Several of my favorite varieties offer exceptional beauty of form and fruit retention in the winter garden. *Malus* 'Red Jade' is a classic weeping form introduced by the Brooklyn Botanic Garden in 1956. Its branches cascade with tiny red fruit. 'Molten Lava' and 'Louisa' also have exceptional weeping forms that stand out against winter snow. 'Louisa' blooms with single pink flowers followed by red fruit and was discovered by Polly Hill of Martha's Vineyard, Massachusetts in 1962. *Malus* ×'Sutyzam', known in the trade as Sugar Tyme, and *M.* ×*zumi* 'Calocarpa' have the most persistent small, red winter fruit. These even last, encased in ice, until the spring flowers open.

Poncirus trifoliata

Malus 'Louisa'

Malus Sugar Tyme

Crataegus viridis 'Winter King'

'Winter King' hawthorn (*Crataegus viridis* 'Winter King') is another small tree with an exceptional winter display. Its broad, spreading crown of branches is horizontal in profile and heavily laden with orange-red fruit. 'Winter King' hawthorn is mostly thornless, with occasional one-and-a-half-inch-long barbs.

Rosa nitida is a native New England rose. Its common name, shining rose, is a reference to its glossy, fern-like foliage that turns a lustrous crimson red in fall. The single pink June-blooming flowers are followed by scarlet-red rose hips that stand out against white winter snow. *Rosa nitida* is a low, two-foot-high, suckering thorny shrub hardy to Zone 3. It is well adapted to growing in a permanent container, which effectively controls its suckers and spreading garden habit.

Cotoneaster, native to China, is a genus of the Rosaceae family. There are many hardy species that have

Rosa nitida

varied growth forms, such as prostrate, low, spreading, and upright shrubs. Some, like bearberry cotoneaster (*Cotoneaster dammeri*), have evergreen foliage. Other species such as *C. apiculatus*, *C. divaricatus*, and *C. horizontalis* are deciduous, with leaves turning shades of red in fall. Rockspray cotoneaster (*C. horizontalis*) grows as a mounding shrub, with its twigs branching in a distinctive fishbone pattern. Showy red fruit is the shared ornamental attribute of the cotoneaster clan.

American cranberry (*Vaccinium macrocarpon*) is Massachusetts' official state fruit. It is hardy to Zone 2. Its native range extends from Newfoundland, Canada south to North Carolina and west to Ohio. Cranberries are truly tough plants, even growing on exposed granite ledge on the coast of Maine, above the crashing surf of the Atlantic Ocean.

A member of the Ericaceae family, cranberry is a trailing evergreen shrub with thin, wiry, branched stems. The bell-shaped flowers are deeply cut into four segments resembling petals, which are turned back to reveal the pistil and stamens. The glossy red fruit, a familiar ingredient often included in Thanksgiving feasts, ripens in the fall. Adding to its late season display are the small evergreen leaves that turn reddish in fall and winter.

Gardens are, by nature, ephemeral. Yet their beauty is expressed through the perpetually changing state of their component parts. Ornamental and persistent fruits add to the garden's aesthetic longevity. Enhance the winter garden's seasonal appeal with a selection of colorful winter berries. Combine these with the sustaining foliage of evergreen shrubs, trees, and groundcovers, as well as winter flowers to create a formula for a long-lived garden experience.

Cotoneaster dammeri

Cotoneaster horizontalis

Vaccinium macrocarpon

Chapter Eight

Persevering Perennials

Herbaceous perennial plants and sub-shrubs that exhibit persistent evergreen foliage and flowers in the winter landscape possess a phenomenal quality. At first glance, this attribute might seem improbable; however, the list of hardy, herbaceous evergreen perennials is quite long. It includes plants with a diversity of sizes and leaf shapes, and the foliar hue of these "wintergreen" gems is an array of colors that ranges from silvery gray to glaucous blue, chartreuse, almost black, and ruddy red.

FERNS AND MOSSES

Verdant mosses are undersung but everywhere, even providing green color for the cracks in asphalt pavement that would otherwise look quite bleak in the middle of winter. I am fond of mosses and have these tough, primitive evergreen plants established on the sunny roof of a garden structure that gets no supplemental irrigation.

Ferns are just one step up the evolutionary ladder from mosses, and evergreen ferns provide a particularly striking presence in the winter garden. Their delicate, pinnately dissected green fronds offer a contrast to the snowy winter landscape. Native ferns include species of *Polypodium*, *Polystichum*, *Dryopteris*, and *Asplenium*.

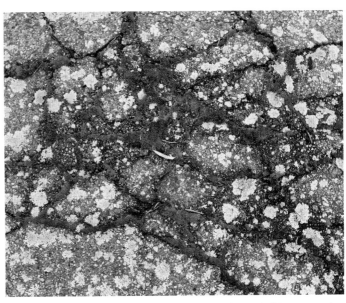

Diminutive mosses add texture and color to even inhospitable pavement.

Polypodium vulgare

Polystichum acrostichoides

Dryopteris marginalis

The common polypody fern (*Polypodium vulgare*) covers shady stone outcrops with mats of evergreen fronds. Christmas fern (*Polysticum acrostichoides*) has arching, evergreen once-pinnate fronds that are larger than polypody ferns. The latter is an easy-to-grow perennial that will sustain sunny conditions as well as partial shade. The feathery, pinnate leaves of Christmas fern are a favorite strong, textural contrast to the stiff, sword-shaped foliage of Adam's needle (*Yucca filamentosa*), striking a surprisingly pleasant combination.

Leatherleaf wood fern (*Dryopteris marginalis*) is another evergreen fern native to northern deciduous woods. Its form is more upright growing than Christmas fern, and it has a clump-forming habit of growth. The fronds of its two-foot-tall, triangular leaves are distinguished by twice-compound pinnae.

Dryopteris erythrosora is an evergreen Japanese species. The cultivar 'Brilliance' has the common name autumn fern, a reference to the copper-pink color of its newly unfurled fronds. Mature leaves of 'Brilliance' are glossy green and form a two-foot-tall spreading groundcover.

Hart's tongue fern (*Asplenium scolopendrium*) is another hardy native evergreen fern. Its leaves have a tropical-looking appearance but are quite hardy, springing up from rocks and crevices. They form a whorl of simple fronds.

PACHYSANDRA

The Japanese carpet box (*Pachysandra terminalis*) shares a common name with its botanical genus: pachysandra. In some gardening circles, it suffers from

Asplenium scolopendrium

an unjustified banal reputation due to its ubiquitous success as a groundcover. This hardy herbaceous member of the boxwood family, Buxaceae, has whorls of evergreen leaves growing eight inches tall. It spreads by rhizome-like stems and forms a dense groundcover in partial shade. Pachysandra can be a noteworthy component of the winter garden.

The cultivar 'Green Sheen' is a truly exceptional beauty. This glossy, lacquered leaf form of pachysandra was selected and propagated decades ago by Connecticut nurseryman Dale Chapman. The leaves of 'Green Sheen' are more lustrous than even the foliage of camellia. Planted beneath winter-blooming witch hazels, it is nonpareil in the wintertime garden.

Pachysandra, similar to many North American native plants, evolved as a separated population with disjunct genera of related species indigenous to Asia. Allegheny spurge (*Pachysandra procumbens*) is native

Pachysandra terminalis 'Green Sheen'

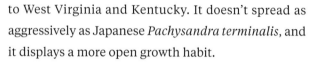

Pachysandra procumbens

to West Virginia and Kentucky. It doesn't spread as aggressively as Japanese *Pachysandra terminalis*, and it displays a more open growth habit.

The gray-green, lightly mottled leaves of Allegheny spurge offer a bold-textured accent combined with evergreen ferns. It is cold hardy far north of its native range. However, in northern gardens, the foliage of Allegheny spurge may not always be truly evergreen.

WANDFLOWER AND OCONEE BELLS

The southern Appalachian Mountains are home to two rare and treasured horticultural gems, wandflower and Oconee bells. "Wandflower," a common name for *Galax urceolata*, is descriptive of its spike-like arrangement of tiny white flowers. Its most desirable characteristic is its evergreen ornamental foliage, and it is a beautiful evergreen perennial I have long admired in a garden far from its southern Appalachian haunts. This slow-spreading perennial forms an elegantly layered colony of three-to-four-inch rounded, glossy leaves.

TOP AND ABOVE *Galax urceolata*

The leaf of *Galax* is somewhat similar to the round form of European ginger (*Asarum europaeum*). Its growth habits and morphological presentation are very different. The foliage of European ginger lies flat; heavy winter snow can make it look even more trodden. *Galax* leaves maintain their elegant, undulating formality throughout winter. A shade-loving perennial, its glossy green leaves take on a bronze sheen depending on their exposure to winter sun. Sadly, this evergreen perennial beauty can be hard to find in the horticultural trade.

The rarity of Oconee bells (*Shortia galacifolia*) is in direct contrast to the prodigious esteem that has been bestowed on this charming wildflower. The discovery of this evergreen perennial sub-shrub is a well documented historical story. It begins with French botanist André Michaux, who in 1787 was plant hunting in the southern Appalachian Mountains, and intertwines with Harvard botanist Asa Gray, who was studying herbaria archives in France in 1839. He called it "perhaps the most interesting plant in North America." Gray came across an unidentified plant specimen from Michaux's expedition fifty-one years earlier. His enchantment with the mystery of the mounted herbarium specimen turned into decades of searching for what he called "the holy grail of plant collectors." A living colony of *Shortia galacifolia* in North Carolina was finally rediscovered in 1877. In 1886, Charles Sprague Sargent of the Arnold Arboretum organized another expedition that was guided by Michaux's field notes. It led to a substantial colony of *Shortia* in South Carolina near the headwaters of the Keowee River. Unfortunately, a contemporary dam, constructed in 1973, destroyed this site. Many plants were saved before the flooding and successfully relocated to botanic gardens and arboreta. The Polly Hill Arboretum on Martha's Vineyard, Massachusetts has an impressive collection that includes a beautiful planting of *Shortia galacifolia*.

The roundish, leathery, glossy green leaves of *Shortia* are held on long leaf stalks. Exposure to winter sun bestows these evergreen leaves with a colorful, transparent red glaze. It is hardy in Zone 5 gardens in New England. *Shortia* is a plant that is illustrative of successful implementation of the practice of preservation

Shortia galacifolia

through cultivation. The support of botanic gardens, specialty nurseries, and dedicated gardeners is essential to saving rare and endangered native species, and with this support, *Shortia galacifolia* and other threatened native beauties will become more commonly cultivated gems in our winter gardens.

VIOLET

A beautiful silver-leafed violet, *Viola walteri* 'Silver Gem', was introduced by the Mt. Cuba Center in 2010, and I was smitten by it when I visited the venerable Delaware botanic garden in mid-October 2012. 'Silver Gem' was selected as a seedling variant from a population of prostrate blue violets endemic to a limited habitat in Alabama. Remarkably, it can withstand Zone 6 cold temperatures. The heart-shaped silvery leaves of 'Silver Gem' have violet undersides. The foliage is quite evergreen and persistent through late fall and into winter. If its prostrate, silver-foliaged carpet of leaves is not completely buried in snow, 'Silver Gem' can add delightful color contrast to the bold green leaves of hellebores. This diminutive violet packs a lot of seasonal punch.

WINTERGREEN

Wintergreen or checkerberry (*Gaultheria procumbens*) is a creeping sub-shrub that forms a low evergreen mat of glossy foliage. It can withstand Zone 3 cold temperatures. Its wide-ranging native habitat extends from Newfoundland, Canada south to Georgia in the high subalpine terrain of the Appalachian Mountains. Both its showy red berries and aromatic leaves are infused with the flavorful oil also known as wintergreen. In the wild landscapes of Maine, it grows in a sunny, hardscrabble habitat of shallow soils atop granite ledges. It is often intermingled with wine leaf cinquefoil (*Sibbaldiopsis tridentata*) and mosses, and its evergreen leaves take on an attractive, ruddy red winter complexion.

Viola walteri 'Silver Gem'

Gaultheria procumbens

CRANBERRY

The tiny evergreen leaves of cranberry (*Vaccinium macrocarpon*) have a similar red-flushed winter-foliage coloration. Like wintergreen, it is a member of the Ericaceae botanical family. Cranberries are a vining sub-shrub with ground-hugging stems that form low, evergreen mats. They grow in well-drained, though moisture-retentive, organically rich soils. The native eastern range of *Vaccinium macrocarpon* extends from Newfoundland, Canada, south to New England. It can withstand Zone 2 cold temperatures, and its tart red berries have a long and storied ethnobotanical history. The first instance of commercial cranberry cultivation occurred in 1816 in the town of Dennis on Cape Cod, Massachusetts. Growing cranberries remains a vital market share of Massachusetts' agricultural economy.

I find the red winter foliage color of commercial cranberry bogs to be surreal and fascinatingly beautiful. Yet it is the charm of cranberries growing on Maine's rocky coast that has provided the inspiration for some of my gardens. The configuration of seaside granite ledges, weathered and fractured from glaciation, is made up of irregular niches that hold shallow pools of rainwater. Lowbush blueberries (*Vaccinium angustifolium*), crowberry (*Empetrum nigrum*), sheep laurel (*Kalmia angustifolia*), tussocks of grasses, mosses, and cranberries rim the water's edge in this garden-like wild landscape. It is a culturally harsh habitat. The shallow, mineral soils are rich with sphagnum and humus and hold dependable moisture, which suits the growth needs of cranberries. They also thrive in a sunny garden setting with a silt-loam soil amended with compost. Installing a subsurface rubber liner allows for cranberries to be grown in an unirrigated garden with dry, sandy loam soil. It mimics the soil moisture conditions found in a naturally occurring, high groundwater environment.

Vaccinium macrocarpon

Vaccinium macrocarpon with *Chionodoxa luciliae*

GRASSES AND GRASS-LIKE PLANTS

Japanese mondo grass (*Ophiopogon japonicus*) is the common name for herbaceous perennial plants with creeping dark evergreen lance-shaped leaves. One extremely dwarf form is 'Gyoku-ryu'; it can withstand Zone 7 cold temperatures.

A much more cold-hardy species that thrives in New England Zone 5 gardens is *Ophiopogon planiscapus*. It is most commonly seen in the cultivar 'Nigrescens',

A close inspection of *Ophiopogon japonicus* 'Gyoku-ryu' reveals turquoise-blue berries.

Silver leaves of *Veronica spicata* subsp. *incana* 'Silver Slippers' combined with black mondo grass sustains an enchanting winter color effect.

also called black mondo grass, with six-inch-tall, ink-black linear leaves that form an evergreen shadowy pattern in the garden. A layer of stark white snow accentuates the form of these spidery black leaves. The contrasting, bold-textured leaves of hellebores combined with 'Nigrescens' create a smashing perennial winter garden vignette.

Creeping lilyturf (*Liriope spicata*) is closely related to *Ophiopogon*. It has similarly shaped green foliage and a grass-like texture, with eight-inch-long linear leaves that lie in an undulating fashion. This evergreen groundcover is native to southwestern China and hardy to Zone 5. *Liriope spicata* grows best in partial shade, and its foliage makes an elegant winter display beneath the colored stems of red-twig dogwood or trees with ornamental bark.

An evergreen perennial that is in the same botanical family as *Ophiopogon* and *Liriope* is the *Rohdea japonica*, or Japanese sacred lily. Its outline is distinctive in

Rohdea japonica

the winter garden. *Rohdea japonica* is a shade-loving perennial that grows eighteen inches high in clumps of arching, lance-shaped, glossy foliage. Clusters of red berries accent its winter show. The leaves of *Rohdea* are green in winter gardens as far north as the Philadelphia, Pennsylvania area, and it is cold hardy in Zone 5, though not necessarily evergreen without winter protection. A horticulturist friend grows Japanese sacred lily beneath a *Heptacodium* tree in his Boston, Massachusetts garden; however, my potted *Rohdea* are safely overwintered in a cool greenhouse. Another familiar member of this botanical family, Asparagaceae, is *Hosta,* the deciduous-foliaged star of the shady perennial border.

Japanese sweet flag (*Acorus gramineus*) is an evergreen herbaceous perennial native to India, China, and Japan, where it grows in damp and boggy areas. This Asian species has grass-like tufts of narrow evergreen foliage that grow to a height of twelve inches. 'Ogon' is a cultivar with stunning yellow-variegated leaves. The leaf surface of 'Ogon' sweet flag is covered in a shiny waxy cuticle. This protective foliar coating is a characteristic of drought-tolerant plants, and although Japanese sweet flag grows in moist (even waterlogged) soils, it is adaptable enough to thrive in drier conditions. 'Ogon' has flourished for more than a half-dozen years planted in my garden with full sun in a sandy loam soil with minimal supplemental water aside from rainfall. In summer, its yellow blades complement the blue leaves of the grass *Panicum amarum* 'Dewey Blue'. In winter, a painted bamboo feature and the colorful foliage of 'Ogon' sweet flag equally shine.

"Rushes are round and sedges have edges" is a rhyming verse that is helpful in field identification of grass-like plants. Indeed, the leaves of *Carex* species—commonly called sedges—have a V-shaped

The progression of *Acorus gramineus* 'Ogon' through the seasons at Tranquil Lake Nursery

Carex morrowii var. *temnolepis*

Plants with bold-textured foliage provide a terrific foil for *Carex morrowii* var. *temnolepis*, including *Mahonia bealei*.

Carex morrowii 'Ice Dance'

triangular cross-section. Many species of sedge have evergreen foliage and are an attractive addition to the winter landscape. My favorite sedge is *Carex morrowii* var. *temnolepis*, a beautiful and distinctive sedge I first encountered thirty-nine years ago at the United States National Arboretum in Washington, D.C. It was introduced to the arboretum by Barry Yinger when he was curator of the Asian collection there. Also called 'Silk Tassels' sedge, it forms an undulating evergreen groundcover of fine, hair-like leaves streaked with a subtle white line. It is a hardy, elegant, and well-behaved clump-forming sedge for gardens in sun to partial shade.

Carex morrowii 'Ice Dance' has narrow, half-inch-wide arching leaves with an elegant white marginal variegation. This beautiful evergreen cultivar from Japan was selected by Barry Yinger and introduced by Hines Nursery to American gardens in 1996. It is a rhizomatous spreading sedge with arching leaves that grow to a height of sixteen inches. 'Ice Dance' has been given the Missouri Botanical Garden's Plants of Merit Award and the Outstanding Plant Award from the International Hardy Plant Union.

Carex oshimensis is an evergreen Japanese woodland sedge species similar to *Carex morrowii*. The cultivar 'Evergold' is a green and yellow-striped variegated form. A sport mutation of this sedge with solid-yellow leaves is named 'Everillo'. It is a clump-forming variety, with weeping mop heads of golden yellow foliage.

Bunny Blue sedge (*Carex laxiculmis* 'Hobb') is an exceptionally glaucous blue-foliaged cultivar. It was chosen as a seed selection of *Carex laxiculmis* var. *laxiculmis*, which is a glaucous green sedge found in woodlands of eastern North America. Its broad silver blue leaves mature to a height of twelve inches. Bunny

Carex oshimensis `Everillo`

Carex laxiculmis `Hobb`

Blue is a slow-spreading sedge that puts on a distinctive winter garden show. Its foliage is reliably evergreen in the Mid-Atlantic region of the United States.

Ornamental grasses have long been champions in the garden for their multiple seasons of beauty and valuable textural displays when combined with flowering herbaceous perennials. Cultivars of large grasses such as switchgrass (*Panicum*), Asian maiden grass (*Miscanthus*), feather-reed grass (*Calamagrostis*), as well as shorter fountain grass (*Pennisetum*) and Hakone grass (*Hakonechloa*), display many shades of green during summer. Their beauty carries on through autumn and into early winter and offers a significant ornamental presence in the garden.

In the late-garden winter season, most remnant stems and leaves of these grasses have turned shades of tan. Persistent, green-winter foliage is found in bamboos, but only a few other evergreen members of the grass family (Poaceae) are hardy in northern gardens.

Two genera stand out and offer green winter foliage, or to be more accurate, winter blue-green foliage. The fine, eight-inch-high tussocks of blue fescue (*Festuca ovina* var. *glauca*) and the two-foot-tall porcupine-like

Helictotrichon sempervirens `Sapphire`

Festuca ovina var. *glauca* `Elijah Blue`

clumps of blue oat grass (*Helictotrichon sempervirens* 'Sapphire') hold their glaucous-green color throughout winter. Both require full sun and soil with good drainage; they cannot tolerate wet soil in winter. The bold, silver-gray leaves of 'Berggarten' sage (*Salvia officinalis* 'Berggarten') make a striking winter foliage combination with *Festuca ovina* var. *glauca* 'Elijah Blue'.

BAMBOO

Kuma bamboo (*Sasa veitchii*) is well suited to cold climates. Winter temperatures impart a decorative transformation to the foliage of this evergreen bamboo. Its broad, blunt, elliptic green leaves acquire a stark white, wide marginal variegation with the onset of freezing weather. This distinctive green-and-white leaf pattern is beautifully sustained beyond winter, spring, and into the succeeding growing season as new green shoots emerge. This dazzling shift in winter appearance brings a new and vibrant look to the foliage of this shade-loving plant. *Sasa veitchii* grows three to four feet in height, though its size can be reduced

by cutting its culms to the ground in late spring. It is hardy to Zone 5. Cold climates may somewhat suppress this bamboo's rambunctious, spreading nature. A three-foot-deep barrier buried below ground helps to keep bamboo restricted.

CYCLAMEN

A few hardy perennials ignore the usual seasonal pattern of spring emergence and winter senescence. Hardy cyclamen, whose common and botanical names are shared, have evolved to exhibit this curious inverse cycle, sprouting new growth in autumn and going dormant in summer. This unconventional growth pattern gives rise to fresh, new foliage that sustains a winter-long evergreen display. Cyclamen are tuberous herbaceous perennials native to the dry, rocky shrublands around the Mediterranean. The Neapolitan cyclamen (*Cyclamen hederifolium*) is a vigorous species. It is hardy enough to thrive in New England gardens and does not require the winter protection of an alpine house.

Sasa veitchii

Variegated foliage of *Cyclamen hederifolum*

The flowers of *Cyclamen hederifolium* first emerge leafless in mid-September, like tiny pink and white butterflies. Triangular, English ivy-shaped evergreen leaves soon follow. These are distinctly colored silver and white in a variable marbled pattern. I have *Cyclamen hederifolium* growing in partial shade under dwarf bear oaks (*Quercus ilicifolia*). They are planted in well-drained sandy loam soil and lightly mulched with the needles of white pine trees. These environmental factors have readily satisfied their cultural needs. The cyclamen colony is flourishing and even expanding through self-seeding, thanks to the symbiotic service of ants.

Cyclamen coum is another beautiful hardy species that is native from Turkey to Israel. Its rounded heart-shaped leaves are colored silver with a central green emblem in the form of a jagged ivy leaf. This species greatly extends cyclamens' bloom season. In gardens at the Scott Arboretum in Swarthmore, Pennsylvania, *Cyclamen coum* blooms with pink flowers from January to March.

While the foliage of cyclamen is present throughout winter, their long quiescence and seasonal disappearance can leave an awkward summer gap in the garden. Suitably sized neighbors should be grown and integrated nearby; however, they must not overgrow their niche. European ginger (*Asarum euopaeum*), Chinese ginger (*Asarum splendens*), and *Viola walteri* 'Silver Gem' are all suitable companions for cyclamen in the garden.

ARUM

Another herbaceous perennial that takes a break through summer is *Arum italicum*. Commonly referred to as Italian arum, its leaves die and disappear as they succumb to summer dormancy. Unlike cyclamen, which requires well-drained soil conditions, this arum needs moist soil in order to thrive—it is even tolerant of winter-wet conditions. Cool autumn temperatures stimulate its new growth of bold, foot-long

Cyclamen coum

Arum italicum

evergreen leaves. They call out for attention in the winter garden.

Forms of *Arum italicum* subsp. *italicum* 'Marmoratum' have the most flamboyant foliage. The venation of their large arrow-shaped, glossy green leaves is marbled with silver-white variegated designs. Its bold texture stands out against the fine foliage of clipped boxwood in winter. For a long winter display, plant *Arum italicum* in partial shade with evergreen ferns such as *Dryopteris erythrosora* 'Brilliance' and snowdrops (*Galanthus*).

EVERGREEN SOLOMON'S SEAL AND EPIMEDIUM

Evergreen Solomon's seal is a very apt common name for *Disporopsis pernyi*. This Chinese evergreen perennial grows to sixteen inches tall. It has arching stems of alternately spaced lance-shaped leaves arranged in a zigzag pattern. It prefers shady conditions, and its evergreen foliage makes a good winter companion for the heart-shaped leaves of evergreen varieties of barrenwort, also commonly referred to by its botanical name, *Epimedium*. The hybrid cultivars *Epimedium* ×*perralchicum* 'Frohnleiten' and *Epimedium* ×*warleyense* 'Orange Queen' in particular combine well with evergreen Solomon's seal.

Horticulturist, plant explorer, and hybridizer Darrell Probst introduced *Epimedium wushanense* to keen gardeners through Garden Vision Nursery in Massachusetts. This new evergreen species, collected in Sichuan Province, China, sports arrow-shaped, spiny margined evergreen leaves. It calls to mind the foliage of *Mahonia*, epimedium's cousin in the family Berberidaceae. The cultivars 'Spine Tingler' and 'Ninja Stars' are two of Darrell's hybrid introductions that display this spiny evergreen foliage to great effect.

Epimedium ×*warleyense* 'Orange Queen'

BERGENIA

Pigsqueak (*Bergenia crassifolia*), an old-fashioned moniker for an evergreen herbaceous perennial now commonly referred to by its botanical name, has been the subject of garden fashion turmoil since Victorian

Epimedium ×*perralchicum* 'Frohnleiten'

Bergenia ×'Eden's Magic Giant'

times. However, its evergreen beauty in contemporary winter gardens cannot be disputed. Bergenia's bold, leathery foliage is handsome year round. Native to northwestern China and Siberia, it is hardy to Zone 3. It will grow equally well in the sun or shade. Bergenia's leaves add a bold winter accent to any garden; it is especially attractive accompanied by the fine-textured foliage of evergreen sedges and grasses. A number of hybrid cultivars display exceptionally large leaves. Lustrous rosettes of 'Eden's Magic Giant' are twelve inches across and turn bronze in winter.

SPURGE

The purple-leafed wood spurge (*Euphorbia amygdaloides* 'Purpurea') is an evergreen perennial with a fleshy taproot. It demands full sun and well-drained soil and can withstand cold temperatures down to Zone 5. 'Purpurea' forms an eighteen-inch tall, bushy clump. Its lance-shaped maroon-tinted foliage is arranged in whorls on reddish stems. It is not a long-lived perennial but will self-seed when given garden conditions

to its liking. Its regal-colored foliage is a delightful presence in the winter garden.

Euphorbia amygdaloides var. *robbiae* is a less cold-hardy variety of spurge that thrives in Zone 7 and warmer climates. Known by the odd common name of Mrs. Robb's hatbox, it develops mounds of dark green leaves and spreads by stoloniferous rhizomes to form an evergreen groundcover. This spurge will grow in full sun or partial shade but requires well-drained soil.

Euphorbia amygdaloides 'Purpurea'

Euphorbia amygdaloides var. *robbiae*

HELLEBORE

Plants in the collective genus of *Helleborus* are the leading stars for perennial presentation in the winter garden. As a whole, the various hellebore species, their interspecific hybrid strains, and the cloned cultivars of complex crosses cover a range of ornamental attributes. Hellebores thrive in partial shade, and there are species and cultivars that are hardy in gardens from Zone 4 to Zone 9. Bloom time in the winter season always varies with the weather, although the green flowers of stinking hellebore are reliably precocious. The flower colors of hellebore species and hybrids range from deep burgundy and black purple to pastel pink, white, and creamy yellow. Some cultivars have double flowers and petals streaked with green. Hellebores' colorful flower petals are actually bracts, which allows them to last for months.

These perennials' palmately compound evergreen leaves can span a foot across. Stinking hellebore

Helleborus foetidus

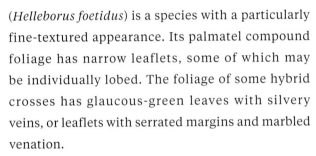

Helleborus niger

Galanthus elwesii

(*Helleborus foetidus*) is a species with a particularly fine-textured appearance. Its palmatel compound foliage has narrow leaflets, some of which may be individually lobed. The foliage of some hybrid crosses has glaucous-green leaves with silvery veins, or leaflets with serrated margins and marbled venation.

The pristine white flowers of Christmas rose (*Helleborus niger*) sometimes bloom at Christmastime in Massachusetts. *Helleborus niger* 'Potter's Wheel' is a renowned selection.

SNOWDROPS

The winter flowers of snowdrops (*Galanthus*) vie for the longest blooming family of hardy herbaceous perennials for the winter garden. This small bulbous herb makes an audacious appearance in the coldest season with seemingly fragile flowers. Nonetheless, these pendulous pearls display endurance and vitality, even blooming through a covering of snow.

Common snowdrop (*Galanthus nivalis*) flowers from January to March. However, the blossoms of other snowdrop species debuted months earlier. Autumn snowdrop (*Galanthus reginae-olgae*) starts blooming in late October and continues through November. Its cultivar 'Rachelae' is a recipient of the Royal Horticultural Society Award of Garden Merit. It is an heirloom form that is referenced in the manuscript of the early twentieth-century garden writer Louise Beebe Wilder as having been collected in 1884 on Mount Hymettus in Greece. The November bloom of *Galanthus elwesii* 'Barnes' is also noted as an honoree of the RHS AGM citation. Another autumnal snowdrop was first introduced to horticultural circles by the Scott Arboretum in Swarthmore, Pennsylvania. *Galanthus elwesii* var. *monostictus* 'Potter's Prelude' has large white, pendulous flowers that first appear in mid-November. These blooms may continue into January.

Snowdrops thrive in a haven where their roots can mingle and intertwine with those of the sheltering deciduous trees and shrubs. They also prefer ground that is lightly layered with leafy mulch. *Galanthus*

ABOVE *Galanthus* ×'Straffan'

RIGHT *Galanthus* 'Lady Elphinstone'

BELOW *Galanthus nivalis* f. *pleniflorus* 'Blewbury Tart'

×'Straffan' is a long-blooming cultivar that produces a second flower scape from each bulb. It is a hybrid cross between *Galanthus nivalis* and the Crimean snowdrop, *Galanthus plicatus*, found at Straffan House in County Kildare, Ireland in 1858. Its floriferous display in horticulturist Jonathan Shaw's New England garden proves that 'Straffan' has stood the test of time. *Galanthus* 'Lady Elphinstone' is another treasured heirloom selection that dates from 1890. It has stunning double flowers with butter-yellow inner petals. *Galanthus nivalis* f. *pleniflorus* 'Blewbury Tart' is a double-flowered snowdrop with a rosette of green petals with a white picotee edge. The expression "cult status" could easily refer to 'Blewberry Tart'; it was discovered in 1975 in the village of Blewbury in Oxfordshire, England.

Other favorites include *Galanthus elwesii* 'Mrs. MacNamara', with large, single, flaring bells above gray-green foliage. *Galanthus plicatus* 'Diggory' is a classic variety that collectors desire. It received the Royal Horticultural Society Award of Garden Merit in 2009. All plant enthusiasts know it is hard to pick a favorite, but the large flowers and vigor of *Galanthus nivalis* 'S. Arnott' give it a discerning nod of commendation.

WINTER ACONITE

Winter aconite (*Eranthis hyemalis*) grows to be about three inches tall, with yellow flowers ringed with a green ruff of palmately cut leaves. A winter cold snap can stunt its emerging growth, reducing plants to a ground-level array of golden balls encased in a sheet of ice. Adversity brings delight.

Horticulturist Jonathan Shaw is a dedicated galanthophile. His Sandwich, Massachusetts garden sustains an incredibly diverse host of snowdrop species and cultivars. In this garden, the flaring buttressed trunks of lofty dawn redwoods (*Metasequoia glyptostroboides*) harbor masses of pearly white snowdrops.

Eranthis hyemalis

The golden yellow flowers of winter aconite (*Eranthis hyemalis*) are a convivial companion to snowdrops.

YUCCA

The morphological quality displayed by yucca foliage calls out for attention. Its best use in the garden is when it is combined with multiple perennials and shrubs with complementing leaves.

Adam's needle (*Yucca filamentosa*) is a stemless broadleaf evergreen shrub that is generally accepted into the category of evergreen herbaceous perennials. It is native not to the desert Southwest, but to the eastern shores of Maryland and South Carolina, south to Florida. *Yucca filamentosa* is winter hardy to Zone 4.

My favorite cultivar is 'Bright Edge', with brilliant yellow margins that outline each green leaf blade. The erect, whorled arrangement of the spiky leaf blades of 'Bright Edge' stands out in the winter garden. Its yellow leaf margins assume a luminous glow when backlit by the low angle of the winter sun. This banded color pattern creates a finer textural impression than the reverse variegated color of the cultivar 'Golden Sword'.

Yucca filamentosa 'Bright Edge' and *Narcissus*

Meld the broad, palmately compound evergreen leaves of Hellebore with the gilt-edged swords of *Yucca filamentosa* 'Bright Edge' and the fine-blue tussocks of *Festuca glauca* 'Elijah Blue' for a verdant winter scene. Lamb's ear (*Stachys byzantina*) has silver-flocked winter remnant flower stems that are topped with spiked whorls of the fuzzy calyx; combine it with the silver-blue needles of *Juniperus squamata* 'Blue Star' and the radial, linear, yellow-striped leaves of 'Bright Edge' with a background of copper-colored, marcescent foliage of *Lindera angustifolia* for a rousing winter garden show. Crowds of the colorful blue flowers of grape hyacinth (*Muscari armeniacum*) carpeting the ground beneath 'Bright Edge' or petite *Narcissus* are a fitting plant combination to herald the return of spring to the garden.

The winter foliage and flowers of evergreen herbaceous perennials contribute tremendously to the beauty and vitality of the winter garden. In the setting of a winter garden, ordinary plants can take on a new significance. Examine and study their form, texture, and color to find the magic within.

Yucca filamentosa 'Golden Sword'

PART III
EMPHASIZING STRUCTURE

Chapter Nine

The Entry Garden

The entry garden sets the tone for gracious hospitality and reception. Its appearance and makeup must be both functional and aesthetically pleasing. Walkways, steps, and landings that lead to the door must be direct, ample, and easy to navigate. A residence's entry is the most frequently traversed destination in the outdoor domain. It should be notable. Wintertime beauty is a requisite for any home that goes through the rhythmic seasons in the temperate zone.

The proportionality of the landscape composition needs to complement the home's architecture and counterbalance it with the site. An entry garden landscape need not shun flowering perennials, shrubs, and trees, but they should be chosen for ornamental qualities that extend over multiple seasons of the year, including winter. Many of the ornamental attributes that are prized for the entry garden are the same criteria used in selecting plants for a winter garden. This includes verdant evergreen foliage, colorful berries, ornamental bark, and of course, cheerful flowers.

Ilex verticillata makes a bold and welcoming statement to visitors in winter.

An entry garden is always on display. Winter is a prime time to appraise it for its structural design, the seasonal beauty of the landscape planting, and for its ability to extend a cordial reception. The residence's door is the primary focal point. The horticultural highlight of the winter entry may merely celebrate a signature plant placed next to it in a container. Or it could be as simple as a spectacular pair of mature winterberry hollies (*Ilex verticillata*) laden with dazzling red berries framing the entry.

I've chosen the following half-dozen entry gardens to use for discussing the intent of each one's landscape design and the analogous selection of plants used to carry out its implementation. They are diverse in their architectural style, materials for constructed walkways, and horticultural palette. These entry gardens, however, all share an aesthetic basis that is sympathetic to the character of place, the genius loci.

COLOR AS THEME

Golden yellow is the gleaming winter color theme for this Westport, Massachusetts entry garden. This cheerful color brightens the garden even on the dimmest days. The chartreuse-colored needles that clothe 'Wate's Golden' pine (*Pinus virginiana* 'Wate's Golden') are echoed in the yellow winter flowers of leatherleaf mahonia (*Mahonia bealei*) planted beneath. Across the entry landing and in view from the kitchen window is fragrant winter-blooming 'Sweet Sunshine' Chinese witch hazel (*Hamamelis mollis* 'Sweet Sunshine'). Its

Hamamelis mollis 'Sweet Sunshine' is a prelude to *Pinus virginiana* 'Wate's Golden' next to this home's front door.

yellow flowers are complemented by accompanying glossy evergreen foliage and gilt fruit of 'Princeton Gold' American holly (*Ilex opaca* 'Princeton Gold').

The entry garden is located several steps below the elevation of the driveway and garage. The form, stature, and position of the 'Wate's Golden' pine provide an important counterbalance to the verticality and scale of the gabled garage wall. A herringbone-patterned elliptical bluestone landing establishes a substantive entry space within the conjunction of irregular house facades. The contrast of the curved perimeter of the ellipse and the angular lines of the stone pattern within give visual weight to the landing space and rivet focus on the entry.

Hamamelis mollis 'Sweet Sunshine' and *Ilex opaca* 'Princeton Gold' continue to echo the golden tones found across the yard.

Pinus virginiana 'Wate's Golden' and *Mahonia bealei* are two plants that anchor the entry's color theme.

Plants are chosen in proportion to nearby architectural features to enhance a sense of good proportion: tall and vertical near the door, low and shrubby under a window.

In addition to the trees and shrubs that embellish it during winter, this garden is also planted with herbaceous perennials and woody shrubs that offer a long and colorful season of bloom. The plants are also chosen for their low maintenance and drought tolerance. The tough beauties that flourish in this entry garden include: Russian sage (*Perovskia atriplicifolia*); bluestar (*Amsonia tabernaemontana* var. *salicifolia*); sea kale (*Crambe maritima*); wineleaf cinquefoil (*Sibbaldiopsis tridentata*); *Hylotelephium* 'Vera Jameson'; Japanese bush clover (*Lespedeza thunbergii* 'Gibraltar'); *Indigofera heterantha*; sweetfern (*Comptonia peregrina*); dwarf sea buckthorn (*Hippophae rhamnoides* 'Sprite'); variegated Adam's needle (*Yucca filamentosa* 'Bright Edge'); Christmas rose (*Helleborus niger* 'HGC Josef Lemper'); and Autumn crocus (*Colchicum* 'Disraeli'). This garden forms a delightful entryway in a sunny terrace space filled with colorful year-round beauty.

Plants with yellow highlights, such as *Crambe maritima* and *Yucca filamentosa* 'Bright Edge' work as a foil to the purple of *Perovskia atriplicifolia* in summer, then accent other yellows as they emerge in fall.

The winter garden of this nineteenth-century home is an excellent case study in the play of light and shadow.

LIGHT AND SHADOW

This home's gabled windows, dark-painted accents, and mix of rich wood and stone textures called for a planting scheme that is equally as dramatic in its play on light and dark. The kitchen entry and the main entrance to the house are distinctly separate in scale, pattern, and construction of their bluestone walkways and steps. Witch hazel is at the top of my list of winter-flowering shrubs for its ability to bestow colorful greetings on all who enter a garden in winter. The flowers of witch hazel combined with the sculptural branching armature of Japanese maples are a key winter feature in this Manchester-by-the-Sea, Massachusetts entry garden.

The driveway border is planted with the evergreen foliage of dwarf inkberry holly (*Ilex glabra* 'Nova Scotia') and the grassy leaves of lilyturf (*Liriope spicata*). Masses of lowbush blueberry (*Vaccinium angustifolium*) display wintry red stems. Combined with prostrate evergreen bearberry (*Arctostaphylos uva-ursi*), they knit together and clothe the ground between outcrops of granite ledge along the entrance drive.

Hamamelis ×intermedia 'Jelena' and *Acer palmatum* 'Katsura' flank the path to the kitchen door. The glossy green needles of *Sciadopitys verticillata* form a spectacular evergreen background for the orange blooms of 'Jelena' witch hazel.

The fine-textured foliage of *Chamaecyparis pisifera* 'Plumosa Aurea Compacta' and *Carex morrowii* var. *temnolepis* is combined with the contrasting bold leaves of *Yucca filamentosa* to accent the entry to the kitchen walkway.

A planter box positioned next to the carriage house features the alluring cerise-red blooms of *Hamamelis japonica* 'Shibamichi Red' and bids a colorful greeting.

A large stoneware pot planted with *Pinus banksiana* 'Schoodic' embellishes the front entry landing. Glossy evergreen leaves of *Sarcococca hookeriana* var. *humilis* and *Buxus sempervirens* 'Justin Brouwers' set off dark colors of the native granite that compose this late nineteenth-century shingle-style facade.

MODERN SHINGLE

The main entry facade of this Woodstock, Connecticut house is oblique to its principal approach. The residence's door is the entry garden's primary focus, although the house facade may not always be in direct sight alignment. Its orientation is at a forty-five-degree angle from perpendicular to the line of the driveway. The walkway design employs a bent axis as a solution that articulates the focus to the main entry.

The front door of the house is recessed within a symmetrical, two-story, tripartite arched loggia. The shelter afforded by the loggia allows for an entry without steps and a doorway threshold that is level with the interior floor of the house. Two flanking facades of the house are skewed at a 135-degree angle from the central entry loggia gallery. The angles produced by the exterior walls of the house and the attached garage form an asymmetric entry court that is enclosed on three sides. A forty-foot-tall tower to the right of the loggia is a striking feature of this house.

The entry walkway, pattered in brick and stone, is generously proportioned. It begins at a right angle to the driveway and terminates on a perpendicular axis

Ilex verticillata 'Aurantiaca' beckons where the entry path bends.

A redbud (*Cercis canadensis*) adds further arboreal winter structure and early spring blooms outside of the kitchen windows. *Arctostaphylos uva-ursi*, *Microbiota decussata*, and *Hakonechloa macra* add plenty of diverse texture.

that is centered on the tripartite loggia gallery. An intermediate, sixteen-foot square parqueted pattern unifies the alignment of the two axes of the walkway. The large scale of the house is counterbalanced by an entry garden that is planted with a number of trees with distinctive branching patterns.

Acer palmatum 'Seiryu' is featured on one side of the loggia. Flanking the doorway are evergreen mounds of 'Tide Hill' boxwood (*Buxus sinica* var. *insularis* 'Tide Hill') and the lobed evergreen leaves of Lenten rose (*Helleborus orientalis*). A grove of several different cultivars of Japanese maple is planted in front of the house facade adjacent to the tower. Beneath them is an evergreen foliage carpet of sweetbox (*Sarcococca hookeriana* var. *humilis*).

The narrow vertical shaft provided by *Liquidambar styraciflua* 'Slender Silhouette' enhances the bent axial lines of the walkway.

The tall form of *Liquidambar* 'Slender Silhouette' establishes a potent focal point that separates the divergent angles of the entry walkway and echoes the vertical lines of the tower. *Magnolia stellata*, transplanted from the owner's former home, was placed across the walk. It counterbalances the scale and anchors the gabled facade of the garage.

A prime consideration for the plants selected for this entry garden, as well as for the entire landscape, is their deer-proof qualities. The durable evergreen leaves of *Buxus sempervirens* 'Vardar Valley' form a horizontal evergreen border that separates the driveway and the entry garden and also echoes the paint trim. The dark green boxwood foliage is also a wintertime foil for the bark of *Magnolia stellata*. Even as here, in March and denuded of foliage, the structure of the plantings feels in balance with the architecture.

CONTEMPORARY FARMHOUSE

The stylistic design of this contemporary house in Weston, Massachusetts is based on the architectural motif of a Japanese farmhouse. This Asian design influence is present throughout the house and is evident in its exterior configuration. The floor-to-ceiling windows that pattern the facade reveal an interconnectedness of interior rooms to the garden space outside. A courtyard garden space is enveloped on three sides by the walls of the house and attached garage. A high stone wall encloses the fourth side. The main entry to the house and garden area is through the masonry wall and along a boardwalk under a roofed pavilion. This restricted access made moving sizable trees into the courtyard, as well as constructing the garden, a challenging endeavor.

A unique and essential element that enlivens this enclosed entry garden is inspired by the sensory experience of sound. In this landscape, the annoying high-pitched sound of distant vehicular highway traffic is almost always present. It permeates private spaces that are meant to be serene. The solution was to buffer bothersome noise by setting up an invisible wall

Inspired by traditional Japanese buildings, a roofed pavilion covers a mahogany boardwalk that leads to the entry door.

A water table glows in early winter, though the rapidly running and falling water doesn't freeze absolutely solid. Flowing throughout winter, the cascading water table generates fascinating ice sculptures. A row of *Vaccinium macrocarpon* lines the near side, changing color dramatically in cooler temperatures. Next to it runs an area filled with *Ajuga reptans* 'Black Scallop' that acts as a buffer between the water trough and walkway.

of soothing sound. The resonant voice of cascading water forms an auricular curtain. It masks the sound of discordant noises in the garden, as well as through open windows in the house.

Reflective and flowing water is a universal and classical component of gardens that has been used for centuries. For this contemporary garden, I designed a sixteen-foot-long water table set two feet above the water surface of a linear pool. It is fabricated from lustrous stainless steel and bronze-tinted plate glass. The water table's horizontal glass surface retains a shallow reflective pool. The water becomes audibly alive by switching on a recirculating pump. Its glassy surface roils and shapes into a shimmering, sheer fluid curtain that plunges loudly into the dark water of the linear pool. In winter, the flow becomes an ice sculpture in its own right.

Designing a garden in a boxed-in space has its conceptual challenges. Its walled demarcation can present both an attractive foil and a discordant distraction. One challenge is that the experience of being in an empty space surrounded by high architectural walls is more oppressive than contemplative. The physical enclosure also makes the space feel much smaller. The discerning placement of trees offers a landscape design solution. Trees counterbalance the architectural scale of walls with their height and form. Their upright trunks and spreading crowns give contrast and relief to the spatial monotony. The vital presence of trees alters and enlivens the static aspect of the enclosed garden, making it feel larger.

A zigzag path of large rectangular stepping stones crosses the garden space diagonally and leads to a side door off the kitchen. The distinctive foliage of *Thujopsis dolobrata* 'Hondai' forms a low evergreen hedge along the length of the main entry facade. Petite glossy leaves of two dwarf cultivars of mountain laurel, *Kalmia latifolia* 'Elf' and 'Minuet', add a different touch of winter greenery. They are combined with several *Chamaecyparis obtusa* 'Gracilis Nana'. The lustrous leaves of *Gaylussacia brachycera* and *Vaccinium macrocarpon* take on a reddish tone in winter.

This enclosed entry garden packs a lot of seasonal punch despite its small size. Its attributes, both horticultural and sculptural, convey a joyful greeting to the homeowners and their guests year-round.

In winter, evergreen trees and shrubs bring verdant structure and life to the garden. The horizontal branches of *Pinus parviflora* 'Glauca' contrast with the vertical frame and pendant branches of *Chamaecyparis nootkatensis* 'Van den Akker'. One pine is planted in concert with a grove of five cedars to compose a dynamic garden background. The differing structures of their green branches camouflage the garage wall, which is in prime view, directly across the garden from the entry pavilion.

The artistic assemblage of conifers forms the perfect foil for the winter flowers and foliage of *Mahonia bealei* and the red winter blooms of *Hamamelis japonica* 'Shibamichi Red'.

WINTER WALKWAY

This entry garden in Westwood, Massachusetts represents the transformation of a narrow, lackluster, alley-like space between the garage and house into a verdant and engaging garden walkway. The main entry door to the house is on a landing directly adjacent to and in view of this redesigned garden space. Its new walkway leads to the kitchen door, a stone terrace, and the garden.

The side facade of the house and side wall of the garage are parallel to each other and just thirteen feet apart. The pitched roof plane of the garage is an aesthetic challenge, making an unattractive view from the kitchen window. The design goals for this entry garden redevelopment were to make this cramped narrow space feel more expansive and welcoming. It also compensates for the dominance of the house and garage facades and ameliorates the view from the kitchen window. The final goal is to create a garden that displays year-round beauty.

The planting is quite simple but very effectively expresses qualitative changes in the mood as well as the physical shape of the space. Significant to the design is the outline of the new stone walkway. It is neither parallel to a wall of the buildings, nor to its own form. Its skewed lines foreshorten the perspective that the symmetrical alignment of the house and garage facades imposes on the space. This arrangement of the walkway makes the space appear to be wider.

An asymmetrical planting arrangement reinforces the optical illusion of proportion. An evergreen cultivar of sweet bay magnolia (*Magnolia virginiana* Moonglow) provides its modest stature, fragrant summer flowers, and luxuriant evergreen foliage

A narrow side yard gets new life.

that fulfill the desired qualities. Choosing trees with a multi-stemmed characteristic strengthens their visual weight to counterbalance the scale of the garage wall. The evergreen treetops of three multi-stemmed magnolias planted along the garage wall obscure its roof and establish a beautiful view through the kitchen window.

The design of the left side of the entry garden, along the garage wall, employs repetition as a design factor. The opposite side has no repetition. It features plants with contrasting foliage textures and colors. Behind a large granite post, the bold, pinnately compound, glossy evergreen foliage of leatherleaf mahonia

The red berries of *Ilex verticillata* 'Winter Red' commingle with the dramatic foliage of *Lindera angustifolia*.

in autumn and remains as copper-colored marcescent leaves in winter.

This entry garden expresses a design concept that illustrates an age-old precept. It showcases the striving for a harmony of contrasts and the intricacy in simplicity.

TRADING TRADITION

Set in the Boston, Massachusetts neighborhood of Savin Hill and overlooking Dorchester Bay, this early-twentieth-century house has details evocative of an earlier shingle-style architecture. Its front entry door is beneath a curved, covered front porch, which faces the bay. Recently, the everyday entry has moved to the rear of the house, with a new hexagonal addition.

The new structure features walls filled with windows that connect the interior space with views of the garden. This new entry is approached up a flight of

(*Mahonia bealei*) and the smooth, fine-textured leaves of Asian spicebush (*Lindera angustifolia*) come together, forming a dramatic harmony of contrasts. The olive-green foliage of spicebush turns pumpkin-orange

When the back of this house became its new entry, a new garden plan ensued.

steps to a wooden deck landing that extends around this new annex to the house. The surface of the deck is built into surrounding retaining walls that are constructed with integrated planting spaces within its structure.

The stark structure of the wall and raised platform initially resembled a bastion fortifying the house. Plants have softened the entry landing, integrating it into the landscape, and transformed it into a delightful entry garden with a secluded sitting area that overlooks the backyard landscape.

Chinese fringe tree (*Chionanthus retusus* 'Tokyo Tower'), a red-flowered 'Diane' witch hazel that is also grown in tree form (*Hamamelis ×intermedia* 'Diane'), and a narrow panel of upright Japanese maples (*Acer palmatum* 'Twombly's Red Sentinel') provide the woody background planted between the ramp wall and a stone terrace. An heirloom cultivar of Boston ivy with tiny lobed leaves (*Parthenocissus tricuspidata* 'Lowii') encrusts the masonry walls with green foliage.

LEFT The garden's planting beds are filled with trees with ornamental winter bark and winter blooms. A dwarf form of Chinese elm with rough-barked branches, *Ulmus parvifolia* 'Seiju', is accompanied by two single-stemmed specimens of *Heptacodium miconioides*.

RIGHT The narrowly upright, weeping form of *Chamaecyparis nootkatensis* 'Van den Akker' occupies a small space between the house and the edge of the property, at the junction of the entry ramp and the far end of the deck. Its key placement screens a view of the neighbor's yard and adds a striking focal point from the kitchen window.

Exfoliating cinnamon-colored bark of *Acer griseum* and *Hydrangea quercifolia* 'Alice' and the red berries of *Ilex verticillata* 'Winter Red' are the wintertime highlights in an adjacent garden bed that extends beyond the outer wall that retains the entry ramp.

Chapter Ten
Views Through Windows and Beyond

Interior spaces with views of the winter garden can be integrated into existing contemporary architecture and gardens. Whether you look to classic garden references or seek inspiration from nature, incorporating plants and gardens into the view from indoors will be rewarding.

VIEWS THROUGHOUT HISTORY

Many extant historical buildings are famously known for architecture deliberately designed to take advantage of garden views from within their interior spaces. This is certainly not a new concept: Some of these structures date back more than eight hundred years. The cultural heritage of these buildings is also quite varied, ranging from a monastery occupied by Benedictine monks to the abode of ancient Chinese scholars, proving that it's a universal desire for humans to sometimes want to be snug inside while looking out over a frozen landscape.

French cloisters first emerged as a monastic style in the twelfth century and continued to be built regularly through the fifteenth. Arcades were built around garden courtyards planted with useful herbal trees, shrubs, and perennials. The Met Cloisters, specifically, is located at Fort Tryon Park in Washington Heights, Manhattan, New York. It is a superlative example of this blend of architecture and horticulture. John D. Rockefeller Jr. financed its construction, which incorporates historic pieces shipped to the United States from elsewhere. Today it's a part of the Metropolitan Museum of Art, which oversees its governance.

This theme of interlinking buildings and garden spaces is also represented in the classical Chinese scholar's garden. These gardens were made as planted sanctuaries to stimulate thoughtful reflection. Roofed pavilions and stucco walls topped with roof tiles at once separate and connect garden spaces to interior rooms. Unique windows designed with elaborate fretwork patterns, called leak windows, frame distinct garden views. Watery reflections and lush greenery are

Cloisters like this one in Toulouse, France often featured open-air arcades with columns and archways that kept people sheltered while providing a view into a planted courtyard.

At the Met Cloisters in New York City, horticultural staff have worked to retain the feel of an original physic, or medicinal, garden in the courtyard.

often contrasted with sculptural stone conglomerations. The views through doorways and windows are purposely aligned through a sequence of differently shaped portals.

You don't have to travel to China to discover the unique architectural framework that extends over a garden paved with geometric mosaic. The Snug Harbor Cultural Center and Botanical Garden (formerly the Staten Island Botanical Garden) includes the authentic, classical New York Chinese Scholar's Garden that opened to the public in 1999; it is based on gardens constructed during the Ming Dynasty. And there are many other examples of this style in public gardens in North America, from Portland, Oregon; Washington, D.C.; and Seattle, Washington; to San Marino, California; St. Louis, Missouri; and Des Moines, Iowa; as well as Vancouver and Montreal in Canada. Many of the elements of style and existentialist design from these ancient gardens can be incorporated into contemporary home gardens.

Fallingwater is a house partially built over a waterfall on Bear Run in Pennsylvania by architect Frank Lloyd Wright. Upon its completion in 1939, its modern design was celebrated as Wright's crowning achievement in organic architecture. Its signature cantilevered terraces extend its interior spaces into the outdoors and look over the stream and waterfalls.

Landscape architect Fletcher Steele was as venturesome a designer as Wright. Steele practiced his innovative skills at the cutting edge of modern garden design. From 1926 to 1958, he collaborated with his client Mabel Choate on a garden terrace built directly against the house at her shingle-style summer home, Naumkeag, in Stockbridge, Massachusetts. From inside the house, it is just a step down and out through glass doors. The fieldstone terrace features a central parterre-knot garden. This is planted with low hedges of boxwood that intertwine, surrounding a shallow, oval reflecting pool of water. A view of the garden can also be enjoyed from an upstairs balcony.

Every element of classical scholar's Chinese gardens, like the Lion's Grove Garden in Suzhou, China, (left and below) is designed to carefully frame what the viewer sees.

Wright used glass walls liberally to open the rooms at Fallingwater to views of the surrounding wooded landscape.

IDEAS FOR CONTEMPORARY DESIGN

These historical references offer much to draw from in incorporating gardens into contemporary homes, especially through winter garden views, and a great many examples are provided in the plant-focused chapters of this book.

Views to the outdoors are a tried-and-true method for bringing a transcendental aspect to the nature of interior architecture. Embellish the interior of your home year-round with these contemplative views of a garden that shines even in winter.

In regions with cold winters, it is especially valuable to plant choice shrubs or trees with ornamental bark in areas that can be seen from inside, especially as inclement weather restricts ventures out into the garden. Small trees can be effectively planted near to walls of single-story houses, as their branches can easily be pruned to accommodate this close placement with no problem. See chapter 4 of this book for more on trees with ornamental winter bark.

The vermillion-red bark of *Acer palmatum* 'Sango-kaku' shows itself off through windowpanes.

SHADOWS AND SILHOUETTES ON SNOW

Deciduous trees provide cool shade in the summer garden with relief from the heat of the sun. Their bare-branched silhouettes can be equally as pleasing to the mood of a winter garden. Trees stand out as sculptures against the winter landscape.

Snow brings a total change to the garden. It magnifies the aesthetics of light and dark lines. Freshly fallen snow still brings out a child-like wonderment in many. A layer of snow is more than a blanket of white that covers the ground—its smooth surface provides a canvas for an impressionistic landscape of shadows. In winter, light interacts with the density of the atmosphere near the horizon. The low angle of the sun makes for engaging winter ephemera of elongated patterns. Compared to those cast on bare ground, the projection of shadows onto snow adds a unique beauty.

Reflectivity defines the visual perception of everything that we see. Though transitory, shadows add a unique beauty to the landscape. If only winter's snow had the longevity to last the entire winter season! In paintings on canvas, shadows and reflections add depth to a subject and create an illusion of three-dimensional space on a flat surface. In the landscape, reflected images and shadow patterns can often mingle.

Those of us living and gardening in snow-prone areas can make use of these silhouettes provided in

The reflective quality of water is a powerful element in the landscape. The mirrored surface of a mere pool can expand the space of a small garden. In winter, its frozen surface remains reflective as well, forming an icy canvas for shadowy silhouettes.

Metasequoia casts an imposing fastigiate silhouette.

Rhus adds a twist akin to modern sculpture.

The rhythm of the regular spacing of an apple orchard is highlighted by a fresh coating of winter snow.

the winter months to assess the basic structure of the garden. Taking a photo of your yard in winter can prove valuable for assessing scale and structure with a fresh eye. And don't forget to plan for how new deciduous trees and shrubs will look when they are bare, or place them purposefully to cast shadows over areas, like summer lawns, that will serve as large blank canvases to add overall painterly interest.

Xanthorhiza simplicissima creates captivating stripes when its mass planting loses its leaves.

Chapter Eleven

The Gestalt
of Groves

The psychology of gestalt tricks our minds into believing that the quality of a configuration, pattern, or group is perceived as more than the sum of its parts. This paradox of mathematical summation is intrinsic and key to the design language of art and music. Negative spaces or pauses between objects or notes are perceived to be an integral component of a composition, not vast swaths of emptiness. These spaces, plus the added dimension of an ethereal bond that resonates between repeated forms, contribute to the gestalt of the overall theme.

This perceived amplification of spatial volume through the mutual interaction of figures is most certainly felt in groves of trees. Groves, bosques, and copses of trees are a familiar theme in gardens from a diversity of cultures, from Asia to Persia, Europe, and North America. Nineteenth-century Massachusetts poet William Cullen Bryant described groves in his poem *A Forest Hymn* as "God's first temples."

When the trees used to make groves also have decorative bark, it imparts structure and lends additional ornamental interest to the winter landscape. Birches are a volunteer species, often the first colonizers of disturbed sites. They establish groves of multi-stemmed trees, amplifying the rhythm of the gestalt motif. The peeling, paper-white bark of birch trunks is unique among other forest trees and has a magical quality, luminescent in dim light. Birch's ethereal white-barked trunks stand out against a background of dark conifers. Combined with the red fruit of winterberry holly (*Ilex verticillata*) and the glossy evergreen foliage of *Leucothoe axillaris*, they make a striking winter display.

Paper birch does grow into a large tree. A denizen of the north woods, it resents summer heat and drought and may not thrive in southern landscapes. 'Heritage' river birch (*Betula nigra* 'Cully') is more heat tolerant. 'Heritage' birch's exfoliating bark ranges in color from creamy white to pink tan. It too is a large tree, growing to sixty feet or more. 'Little King' is a relatively petite form of *Betula nigra* only growing to twenty feet in height. It can withstand judicious pruning to shrink its size significantly.

American beech (*Fagus grandifolia*) is another tree that can be used in a grove. The smooth, finely finished silver-gray bark and elephantine trunks of American beech vie with paper birch for prestige and prominence in the winter landscape. Its assets include beautiful bark and foliage that turns a warm, coppery tan and persists all winter. Beech trees also have a propensity for making snug copses, often sprouting juvenile stems from old trunks and roots. Although beeches grow into majestically large trees, they can also conform to smaller spaces and submit to hard pruning.

One of my ingrained childhood memories from growing up on my family's farm in Maine is exploring the shadowy beech woods that grew on the edge of a hay field. The silver trunks were smooth and unblemished and the forest floor almost bare of undergrowth, carpeted with tan leaves. I planted a postage stamp-size beech grove ten years ago. Twenty-five two-foot-tall American beech seedlings were set out in a grid of five rows, spaced about three feet apart, forming a sixteen-foot square. A decade later, fifteen survivors form a grove eighteen to twenty feet high and as wide. Its intimate size and configuration are mesmerizing—a lilliputian forest mimicking an abstract distillation of the forest primaeval.

The beeches impart a special beauty in winter, with or without a frosting of snow. The low winter sun burnishes the coppery foliage and produces shadows through a skeletal armature of silver-gray trunks and branches. Even in the dead of winter this grove still appears full of energy and life, illustrating how groves can offer a valued addition to even a small garden.

Weeping European beech (*Fagus sylvatica* 'Pendula') may seem an unusual choice for a grove. Yet a most impressive copse of weeping beech commands attention on the historic grounds of the H. H. Hunnewell Arboretum near Boston. Around 1860, a rare specimen of European weeping beech was planted. The copse evolved as the tree grew, its pendulous branch tips touching the ground, rooting, and proceeding to sire a novel ring of adventitious trees with vertical trunks and arching branches. This beech grove forms a soaring cathedral-like space, with columns rising up and vaults arching down. The beech's architectural motif formed by the massive gray trunks is a fanciful version of stalagmites and stalactites. The original, central tree has died, yet the unique grove that formed over time is a horticultural tour de force representing the height of gestalt. A configuration well worth emulating.

Bringing the theater of groves in close proximity to a house blends architecture into the landscape. I planted a grove of three American hornbeam (*Carpinus caroliniana*) within a stone terrace close to the house. A native small tree found growing in the woodland understory, American hornbeam is tolerant of partial shade. It has sinuous gray bark that covers distinctive muscle-like ripples in its trunk and branches. This characteristic gives meaning to hornbeam's common name of "musclewood."

Heptacodium miconioides is a small tree with a fountain-shaped habit. Its botanical name, *Heptacodium*, and the English translation of its Chinese common name, seven-son flower, both refer to its flowers, which are arranged in whorls of seven. These open in September, an autumnal display of clusters of fragrant white flowers adorning branch tips. After the petals have dropped, *Heptacodium* puts on a stellar encore performance in October with a striking array of rose-red calyces that persist into November. *Heptacodium* also has a winter presentation: Its trunks and branching armature are covered in a conspicuous,

Birches are forest icons that have inspired artists, both in prose and works on canvas. They make excellent groves.

pale tan-colored bark, loosely exfoliating in shredding layers.

Groves of trees can be planted in random repetition or in a frame of rectilinear geometry. I planted a grove of six *Heptacodium* in a uniform grid pattern, echoing the porch colonnade that overlooks the garden. Under each tree in the grid is a meadow-like matrix of *Carex morrowii* var. *temnolepis*, *Helleborus orientalis*, *Geranium* 'Rozanne', and autumn crocus (*Colchicum autumnale*). This garden is designed with plants selected to showcase the colorful richness of fall and winter. No one is home to appreciate summer flowers—they've all gone to the beach. The garden shrugs off and survives summer abandonment with no automated irrigation system. It comes into its colorful prime in September when the *Heptacodium* start to

bloom. Accompanying them are asters, autumn crocus, Asian bush clover (*Lespedeza thunbergii* 'Gibraltar'), and witch hazel (*Hamamelis virginiana*). These are followed by the red fruits of *Malus* 'Molten Lava' and winterberry holly (*Ilex verticillata*), red twig dogwood, orange and coppery foliage of *Lindera angustifolia*, and evergreen variegated whorls of *Yucca filamentosa* 'Golden Sword'.

The regular cadence of the light-colored forms of *Heptacodium* gives greater focus to the grove against the randomness of the woodland beyond. Several conifers, including a dwarf contorted form of weeping white pine (*Pinus strobus* 'John's Find') break the regularity of the grid, adding evergreen sculptures. The chrome yellow needles of *Pinus virginiana* 'Wate's Golden' gives additional warmth to this winter garden.

A key component to the allure of groves is rhythmic repetition. This is often expressed in the multiple use of the same tree variety. The pastoral paradigm of orchards, with one type of tree repeated in uniform regimentation, comes to mind. A novel variation in composing groves is to reiterate similar characteristics common to unrelated tree species. This theme is artistically achieved in the Monk's Garden at the Isabella Stewart Gardner Museum in Boston. The grove lauds trees with colorful trunks, a collage of mottled and exfoliating bark. This historic garden space was designed by landscape architect Michael Van Valkenburgh.

The exfoliating reddish brown to tan mottled bark of *Stewartia pseudocamellia* accompanies the peeling cinnamon bark of paperbark maple (*Acer griseum*) and the white trunks of gray birch (*Betula populifolia*) to make up the grove's trio of performers. A convoluted, coiling, graphite colored brick path binds the multitude of trees together and invites exploration. This sense of movement and rhythm magnifies the narrow courtyard space, enclosed on three sides by the museum facade and a high brick wall. The Monk's Garden evokes gestalt.

I find the Monk's Garden particularly stimulating in winter. The grove's colorful, ornamental bark comes into riveting focus, not obscured by foliage. The grove of trunks is also accentuated by a verdant evergreen groundcover composed of Christmas rose (*Helleborus niger* 'HGC Josef Lemper'), bear's foot hellebore (*Helleborus foetidus*), Chinese wild ginger (*Asarum splendens*), Christmas fern (*Polystichum acrostichoides*), and Autumn fern (*Dryopteris erythrosora* 'Brilliance'). *Helleborus niger* often blooms with single white flowers by late December, followed by the distinctive greenish flowers of *H. foetidus* and white nodding heads of *Galanthus*. Evergreen sentinels of fastigiate arborvitae

(*Thuja occidentalis* 'Hetz Wintergreen') punctuate this deciduous grove, adding visual weight.

Paperbark maple, birch, and *Stewartia* are just the beginning of the list of trees with beautiful winter bark. Persian ironwood (*Parrotia persica*) is another gem with striking mottled bark to add to the winter garden. This tree's fall foliage turns orange late in the season and can persist into winter. I planted a long curving grove of *Parrotia* and underplanted it with *Buxus sempervirens* 'Vardar Valley' and yellow root (*Xanthorhiza simplicissima*): a drought-tolerant and deer-proof combination.

Dawn redwood (*Metasequoia glyptostroboides*) is a deciduous conifer with colorful reddish brown bark and a distinctive winter profile. It's notable for its symmetrical pyramidal form, with radiating branches from a tapered bole. Dawn redwood's flared and furrowed, buttressed trunk anchors its towering height. Often associated with ancient temples in China, it is well suited for being planted in groves. Majestic groups of these closely spaced trees are a beautiful part of the collections at the Morris Arboretum and Gardens in Philadelphia and the United States National Arboretum in Washington, D.C. An ancient species once only known from fossil records, it has become a versatile staple of modern landscapes, even as an urban street tree. A monumental one-and-half-mile-long avenue planted with an allée of five hundred dawn redwoods is a major tourist attraction in Makino, Japan.

Planted in close fellowship, the geometry of dawn redwood's crown adapts artistically. An allée of dawn redwood at the Scott Arboretum on the campus of Swarthmore College in Pennsylvania may not rival Japan's showstopper, yet is impressive nonetheless. The regiment of buttressed trunks stands firm against drifts of snow and forms a haven for a planting of evergreen *Dryopteris*, *Rohdea japonica*, *Arum italicum*, and winter flowering *Galanthus*. You'll also find dawn redwood among the conifer collection at the Arnold Arboretum of Harvard University in Jamaica Plain, Massachusetts, including an unusual, multi-stemmed specimen. This unique tree has five trunks rising from a single base, as if sprouting from a coppice. It forms an unparalleled grove soaring to heaven. A playful hand in fashioning *Metasequoia* groves can also be seen at the Donald M. Kendall Sculpture Gardens at PepsiCo global headquarters in Purchase, New York, designed by Russell Page.

Following the adage "imitation is the sincerest form of flattery," I planted multiple dawn redwoods in a closely spaced grove, as close as five feet apart. If it lends a sculptural background even at a tender age, imagine it in a half century.

Fastigiate forms of evergreen conifers also make dynamic, magical groves. They should be adequately spaced to avoid growing together into a monolithic hedge. It is the spaced rhythm that gives groves gestalt. *Thuja occidentalis* 'Hetz Wintergreen' grown as a single-stemmed tree is one of the hardiest conifers to mimic the narrow spires of non-hardy Monterey cypress. *Thuja occidentalis* 'DeGroot's Spire' is similar, but smaller. Trees that grow as very narrow columns do not become out of proportion as they grow taller, thus maintaining a harmony of scale even in small spaces. A grove of columns (even the towering boles of *Metasequoia*) transfigure a space into vertical shafts of light and shadow.

In winter, a grove of trees is distilled to its skeletal armature, invigorating the winter landscape with the interplay of trunks, branches, and shadow. A grove can transform many parts of your landscape, greeting you daily as a key feature of an entry garden or a view from your kitchen window. Contemplate its gestalt.

Thuja occidentalis 'DeGroot's Spire' is a fastigiate tree that works well planted as a grove, if allowed space.

Chapter Twelve

Fastigiate Forms

Modest footprints have a big impact. The columnar form arises from a small base, attracting attention to itself. It creates a focal point in the landscape. It literally forms an exclamation point and deftly defies Newton's laws of motion. In a sense, the principles of art in garden design overrule the physical law of dimensional analysis—in the landscape, a figure's mass transcends its dimension. Thus, in practical use, a columnar plant has the physical bearing to counterbalance much larger objects and vistas.

A classic example of the power inherent in fastigiate forms is found on the National Mall in Washington, D.C. This monumental landscape is laid out on an axis, stretching two miles from the US Capitol to the Lincoln Memorial. The focal point that rivets attention and holds this monumental landscape in abeyance is the Washington Monument. This 555-foot-tall obelisk punctuates the sky and holds attention for miles; it is truly a powerful vertical form. The marble shaft does more than dominate the vastness of the National Mall; it also augments space by effectively dividing the linear vista of the Mall. It controls the whole view while occupying a relatively small footprint. It establishes a clear foreground and background, making the landscape appear even larger.

The idea of making a space appear larger by partitioning it into smaller units may sound incongruous. However, this abstract design conceit works because the slimness of the vertical object does not visually obscure the whole space, even as it acts as a visual stop. A space that is divided by a vertical object appears larger than one defined only by its perimeter.

No matter the size of the garden, the use of fastigiate forms can provide an essential foil to make small spaces seem bigger and give counterbalance to large spaces. Tall, skinny trees have more applications than just filling narrow spaces. Used judiciously in the broader landscape, they enliven and enlarge our gardens, optically forging new space.

The winter garden requires special design skills. It is crucial to infuse vitality into a garden that is no longer actively growing. In spring and summer, herbaceous perennials, deciduous shrubs, and trees grow exuberantly, channeling energy into luxuriant foliage and colorful flowers that add depth and focus to the garden. Winter strips away much of this richness. The use of different vertical plants creates contrast in the garden's ground plane. These forms also stand out in drifting snow and add structural bones to the garden. They provide contrast and focus, exuding energy and bringing verve to the winter garden.

Vertical forms can be used singularly or as a repeated rhythm. Planting in matched pairs can be appealing, but it is static. Asymmetry conveys movement and a kinetic sense of energy that is especially valuable in a frozen winter landscape. Vertical plants are not inherently emblematic of a certain design or style of garden. The vertical Mediterranean cypress (*Cupressus sempervirens*) is the most recognizable conifer in southern Europe and western Asia. Its imposing, narrow profile frequently distinguishes Mediterranean or Italianate gardens. In New England, Mediterranean cypress is not hardy, but fortunately, we have a varied selection of regionally hardy conifers and deciduous trees with svelte forms that offer comparable vertical architectural interest.

A pyramidal coniferous tree known as eastern red cedar (*Juniperus virginiana*) can be found from southern Maine to South Dakota, south to northern Florida, and southwest to Texas. Furthermore, its profile can vary from broadly conical to narrowly columnar. One columnar cultivar, *Juniperus virginiana* 'Taylor', has been widely propagated and disseminated in the ornamental horticulture domain. It was introduced in 1992 by the Nebraska Statewide Arboretum after it was found growing in the wild near Taylor, Nebraska. This cultivar creates an impressive focal-point column. Like

other red cedars, it grows best in full sun and is quite drought-tolerant.

The northern white cedar, familiarly known as arborvitae (*Thuja occidentalis*), is another common pyramidal conifer. It has a rather restrained native range compared to its red cousin. Arborvitae likes cooler climes, growing as far north as the Arctic tree line in Canada. It is indigenous to forests throughout the Great Lakes region, east through New England, and south along the higher, colder elevations of the Appalachian Mountains to North Carolina. But arborvitae's

Juniperus virginiana 'Taylor'

ubiquitous presence in horticulture defies the selective scope of its native habitat. Much of its innate beauty is lost through inept pruning practices and crude misplacement in residential landscapes. Often known pejoratively as a hedge plant, there are exceptional forms of arborvitae for the winter garden. The singularity of vertical *Thuja occidentalis* cultivars grown as single-stemmed trees is a thing to be celebrated.

I have long been fond of 'Douglasii Pyramidalis' for its slender, columnar form and the upright fern-like whirl of its foliage. This variety has been cultivated since 1891, though it has become scarce in the contemporary nursery industry. Perhaps surpassing it is 'DeGroot's Spire', an exceedingly distinctive cultivar introduced in 1980. Its compact growth forms a fastigiate column recognized for its rough-textured outline and upright, twisted fern-like foliage. Tall, robust 'Hetz Wintergreen' is a narrow, upright cultivar that originated as a seedling selected in the 1940s by a Pennsylvania nursery. It is an excellent choice to mimic the Mediterranean cypress, especially grown to a single trunk. 'Brobeck's Tower' is a dwarf variety of this columnar group. All thrive in full sun and moisture-retentive soil. Unfortunately, they are fodder

Thuja occidentalis 'DeGroot's Spire'

Thuja occidentalis 'Hetz Wintergreen'

Buxus microphylla var. *japonica* 'National' (left) and *Taxus ×media* 'Stricta' (right)

for deer, so preventative measures are necessary to preclude devastating damage.

Plants with vertical forms have individual personalities and unique attributes aside from their erect posture. Narrow, upright forms of boxwood and yew are the epitome of green garden columns. The finely textured leaves of the former and the black-green needles of the latter complement their refined architectural form. Both are culturally versatile and will grow in full sun as well as in shade. Unfortunately, yew is also deer candy, though a scrim of black netting is quite innocuous and offers discreet protection for these noble evergreens. Its many narrow forms include English yew (*Taxus baccata* 'Fastigiata') and cultivars hybridized with Japanese yew (*Taxus ×media*), which are notably cold-hardier. The venerable Vermeulen Farm and Nursery in New Jersey introduced numerous superb vertical selections of those hybrids, such as 'Beanpole', 'Flushing', 'Pilaris', 'Robusta', 'Sentinalis', 'Stricta', and 'Viridis'. Some of these notable cultivars have become scarce in the retail nursery trade, though many mature columnar specimens can still be found in botanic gardens and arboreta.

Buxus sempervirens 'Graham Blandy' is the most common columnar form of boxwood. It may be preferable to yew if deer are a problem, as they find it unpalatable. Both vertical forms of yew and 'Graham Blandy' boxwood benefit from tight pruning to prevent possible ruinous damage from heavy, wet snow. Cinching the plants with a corset of sisal twine before winter is also prudent. Both are also effective as garden sentinels, used to signal a change in direction, a stop before a set of stairs, or the beginning or end of a path. They also add height to a mixed perennial border without taking up much space. Delicate vines such as clematis and tall, lax perennials affectionately embrace their frame.

Pairing the emphatic design principles of repetition and sequence with the canon of contrast makes for a dynamic garden that is lively even in winter. I used 'Graham Blandy' boxwood in this way, offering a repeated note, echoing its form across six plants spaced in an arc. It makes a sinuous curve of vertical green posts. These boxwoods contrast starkly with the blocky stone wall in the background. A seventh boxwood sentinel stands opposite, adding unity and balance—it is a harmony of contrasts. The staccato theme repeats in the vertical boxwoods, and the horizontal line of the stone wall is repeated through the imaginary line formed by their apex. In summer, brightly flowered perennials and annuals mingle through the boxwood staves.

Buxus sempervirens 'Graham Blandy' also played a starring role in making a dramatic entrance to a new garden. The site for this garden is an acre-size flat parcel with an existing stone wall separating it from the rest of the property. We started by changing the straight line of the boundary wall, folding it like an origami figure into a sequential series of five zigzag segments to create six apertures for the new garden. The perpendicularity of the new zigzag wall pattern exposed eight facets of each wall segment, greatly increasing vertical corners and a sense of vertical repetition. Five vertical evergreens demarcate the openings between each zigzag wall, including one *Thuja occidentalis* 'DeGroot's Spire' and four 'Graham Blandy' boxwood. A further accent is provided by a line of dwarf crabapples (*Malus sargentii* 'Tina') set parallel to the vertical evergreens at the end of each wall segment. These crabapples are top-grafted onto

vertical trunks that show off their horizontal branching. *Mahonia bealei*, with glossy, coarse-textured evergreen foliage, and *Helleborus orientalis* are planted in the corners of the walls. The resulting entry garden is full of reverberation, staccato rhythm, and syncopation, as lively as Ravel's *Bolero*. It rouses attention even in the still depths of winter.

Weeping Alaskan cedar (*Chamaecyparis nootkatensis* 'Pendula') can be found in several cultivars with varying degrees of swag. 'Green Arrow', an upright weeping selection, is markedly narrower than 'Pendula', with open recurved branches and pendant secondary branchlets. 'Van den Akker' is an anomalous assemblage of drooping evergreen fronds festooned on an erect bole. This polarity of upright and pendulous habit creates a cartoon-like, exaggerated demeanor, with swooping, animated arms like humanoid trees of pop culture. My landscape client smiles whenever she's greeted by the grove of 'Van den Akker' in her entry garden. This cultivar will grow in full sun as well

Buxus sempervirens 'Graham Blandy'

Buxus sempervirens 'Graham Blandy' installation and throughout the seasons

as substantial shade—I also have a grouping planted directly under the canopy of a large pin oak.

Weeping white spruce (*Picea glauca* 'Pendula') is a green column with stiffly pendant branches, conforming to a space as narrow as a utility pole. Spruce's fine-textured needles are markedly different from the coarse foliage of *Chamaecyparis* and *Thuja* and appear smooth. 'Pendula' mimics the picturesque, spire-shaped form of spruce and fir found in harsh mountainous environments, or the blustery rock-bound coast of Maine. In these environments, this form is adapted to shed snow and shrug off winds, and 'Pendula' also sheds snow easily. I find it particularly attractive in multiples, groups, and groves, and I used the paradigm of Maine's Acadian spruce forest

in an entry garden. A grove of *Picea glauca* 'Pendula' is planted with a groundcover of lowbush blueberry (*Vaccinium angustifolium*) and the glossy evergreen box huckleberry (*Gaylussacia brachycera*). Like most spruce, it requires full sun.

A grove of this vertical spruce also worked well in the design for a postage stamp-size city garden, making a big impact in a tiny space. The trees' collective evergreen spires impart focus and add depth to the small garden and divert attention away from its fenced perimeter.

One more fastigiate conifer of note is weeping Serbian spruce (*Picea omorika* 'Pendula'). Like its weeping brethren, its branches conform tightly to its trunk, making it quite resistant to snow and ice damage. The

Chamaecyparis nootkatensis 'Green Arrow'

Picea glauca 'Pendula'

pair pictured, planted at the Arnold Arboretum in Boston, appear as twin evergreen steeples.

There are many fastigiate forms of deciduous trees. Vertical masts are formed by narrow, upright cultivars of hornbeam, beech, oak, and sweetgum. Planted singly, they mimic the image and intent of the Washington Monument. This role is filled by 'Slender Silhouette' sweetgum (*Liquidambar styraciflua* 'Slender Silhouette') in an entry garden, a key design element that both provides focus and augments space.

Picea glauca 'Pendula' fit well into this tiny urban garden.

Picea omorika
'Pendula'

Liquidambar styraciflua 'Slender Silhouette'

Its position acts as an abstract fulcrum that visually punctuates the alignment of the walkway's bent-axis pattern, and its slim, vertical form echoes the house facade's tower. It also strongly demarcates a spatial foreground and adds depth to the garden. Moreover, the beauty of this design is not lost in winter. The effect of denuded branches in the snow magnifies the garden's structural beauty.

The repetition of vertical forms can create a focal point with an overall appearance that is the inverse of the shape of each individual tree. This qualitative change is represented by a grouping of seven closely planted fastigiate oaks, *Quercus ×warei* 'Long', which carry the trade name Regal Prince. These vertical oaks are a finale to a garden area leveled on a steep hillside. This composition of reiterated upright forms counterintuitively modulates into a horizontal plane, giving the garden a focused ending. The oaks also add a harmony and balance to the steep incline of the site, and their profiles are handsome in the muted, snowy

winter landscape. The level lawn is bordered by a horizontal blue line of *Juniperus squamata* 'Blue Star', which leads to the vertical curtain of oaks.

In a garden in an open, rolling rural landscape, I used a combination of coniferous and deciduous vertical forms to provide direction, balance, and focus. I designed a square ten-foot-tall timber frame as an architectural reference to the Georgian colonial house, which dates to the 1750s. This equilateral frame is positioned on an axial line that emanates from the house ell, forming a level portal through a rambling agrarian wall that separates the garden from a field beyond. The level top of this square portal echoes the

horizontal branching of a mature white pine (*Pinus strobus*) in the background. The exfoliating, reddish barked trunk of paperbark maple (*Acer griseum*) is also framed by the uniform structure.

A fastigiate beech (*Fagus sylvatica* 'Dawyckii') sets off the lineal progression of erect, vertical forms. It is followed by the drooping, branched 'Green Arrow' Alaskan cedar. A third form, weeping Serbian spruce, is triangulated to complement the beech and cypress set against the stone wall. This triad of trees visually anchors the garden's foreground in focus and balances it against the scale of the open, amorphous scene beyond the wall. Blanketed in the whiteness of winter

OPPOSITE AND ABOVE *Fagus sylvatica* 'Dawyck Purple' (left) with *Chamaecyparis nootkatensis* 'Green Arrow' (right)

snow, the differentiated vertical structure of these trees, combined with other forms in the garden, gives life to winter's stillness.

Try to contemplate your garden's composition in winter in this way. Study the lay of the land and the orientation and azimuth of the wintertime sun. Be deliberate in taking into account the patterns that nature offers in your garden's design, and emphasize them with the singular impact that fastigiate forms can impart.

Chapter Thirteen

Clipped, Pleached, and Espaliered Shapes

ighlighting the structural composition and ornamental forms of trees and shrubs is fundamental in making an enduring winter garden. Once the luxuriance of flowers and foliage has been stripped away and plants become quiescent, the vital essence of the winter garden is very much aligned to an emphasis on structural design themes. In other words, the style and organization of the garden's bones becomes very evident in winter.

Creating clipped hedges of evergreen shrubs, pleached panels of deciduous trees, and espaliers of woody plants trained on walls infuses an energetic life into the winter garden. The artistic use of secateurs plays a significant role in the implementation of this endeavor.

Topiary at Longwood Gardens in Kennett Square, Pennsylvania

HEDGES

The best gardens, regardless of season, size, or intricacy, are often laid out with an eye that is partial to simplicity as well as rhythmic recurrence. In the winter garden, a well-executed evergreen hedge offers a simple solution that maintains the garden's accent of pattern and structural integrity. The natural forms of an individual boxwood, yew, or holly all have their own innate beauty. However, a uniformly clipped and pruned architectural hedge made up of an amalgamation of many plants magnifies their beauty. Pruning plants into a hedge is more than just transformative. The hedge's uniform structure also gives focus and defines the garden with a measured outline. Its regularity also acts as a complement to the random natural forms nearby. Depending on its placement in a garden, a hedge may appear as a monotonous border or as a stimulating textural counterpoint.

SAKONNET GARDEN

The exquisite yew and boxwood hedges at Sakonnet Garden in Rhode Island are extraordinarily pruned. The garden's artistic air reflects the expert design, cultivation, and masterful pruning skills of gifted horticulturists John Gwynne and Mikel Folcarelli. The garden is both sophisticated and playful. The sheared panels of yew and boxwood impart a subdued elegance to its ebullience. The enclosed garden at Sakonnet is a maze of interconnected rooms. It offers an "Alice in Wonderland" experience of contradistinction. Stooped over to enter through a modest portal in a clipped boxwood hedge, you instantly crane your head back to look up to the straight, soaring shafts of tree trunks that form a small woods. The closely spaced, naked, reddish-barked trunks of Japanese cedar (*Cryptomeria japonica*) form an allée that flanks a boardwalk path. This narrow passage, dappled with light and shadows from the cedar trunks, is a preview to a magical garden venture. Passing through the sequential Japanese cedar grove, the garden's spatial quality radically shifts from the vertical to the horizontal. An intimate garden that is minimally planted follows; its form is an open quadrilateral of lawn. A sun-filled greensward, it is offset with facing dark rectangular panels of finely clipped yew hedges. It is an elegant, verdant room; the stillness of the space

is mesmeric. The garden evokes the art of Mondrian's Cubist modernism. The black-green winter color of the clipped panels of yew plays in stark surrealistic contrast to the snowy white ground.

The main axial course continues onward to a perpendicular path intersection and a circular finale. In summer, this enclosed oculus is boisterous with mingled layers of chartreuse foliage and flowers. The winter scene is much quieter, though still captivating. The chartreuse leaves of *Hakonechloa macra* 'Aureola' have bleached to tan wands that arch and protrude through the snow. With the golden filigreed leaves of 'Goldenvale' ghost bramble (*Rubus cockburnianus* 'Goldenvale') gone, their chalk-white barbed stems are now exposed to show off their wiry form that contrasts with the green, smoothly clipped boxwood hedge.

A sentry of several paperbark maples (*Acer griseum*) stands outside this sheared circle. Sakonnet Garden's bones—its arrangement of ornamental trees and amazing clipped evergreen hedges—set the stage for summertime lavishness, and indeed, the garden's horticultural zenith indisputably arises throughout the spring and summer months, when rhododendrons bloom and an abundance of herbaceous exotica flourish. Yet these bones also enhance the winter season with panache.

THE BOUNTY OF BOXWOOD

Boxwood (*Buxus* spp.) is a versatile and invaluable evergreen for winter. Its fine-textured, shiny green leaves add a freshness to the winter garden. Thriving in full sun, boxwood is also tolerant of growing in dry

ABOVE A *Taxus* hedge aptly defines an outdoor room in winter and feels akin to Cubist modernism.

LEFT This circular garden is enclosed by a stunningly slender, tall, and tapered curved boxwood hedge.

In summer this garden features fragrant and colorful flowering herbs planted within the boxwood hedges and stone structures that maintain their character even in winter.

shade, making it an indispensable choice for planting under trees. It is also quite unappetizing to grazing deer. My favorite boxwood is also one of the hardiest, to Zone 4: the cultivar 'Vardar Valley'.

Buxus sempervirens 'Vardar Valley' was found growing in the Balkans in 1935 and introduced into America by the Arnold Arboretum in 1957. It forms a spreading mound of dark green foliage, and its blunt, rounded leaves don't have the unpleasant odor often associated with boxwood.

Buxus sempervirens 'Newport Blue' is a compact upright form with a distinctive glaucous blue cast to its leaves. A fifty-year-old specimen in my garden is over eight feet tall. However, like most boxwood, it also lends itself to judicious pruning that greatly moderates its size.

TOPIARY

Topiary is the most prodigious exercise in pruning. It's a horticultural indulgence that has been practiced for millennia. Though ancient in expression, topiary endures a turbulent fashion history and has been in

Evergreen boxwood hedges also sustain the beauty of this entry garden through winter, even in depths of snow.

The winter scene of glossy green foliage is enhanced by the mottled bark of *Stewartia pseudocamellia*.

The zigzag hedge and *Stewartia* provide structure and interest in both summer and winter.

The uniformity of this series of slender evergreen pillars, seen from both sides, mirrors the horizontal plane of the wall.

and out of vogue over the centuries. Suffice to say, topiary's interpretation of geometric forms is playful and fun. It is especially valued in winter, when spheres, obelisks, and multi-tiered disks are coated in a confection of snow.

The first and oldest topiary garden to be planted in the United States continues to thrive and still engages quizzical stares and admiring smiles. It was established in 1854 as the Italianate Garden at the H. H. Hunnewell Arboretum near Boston. Its topiaries are arranged on a hillside overlooking a lake, perhaps a salute to Lake Como in northern Italy.

These topiaries are made of northeast native conifers: white pine (*Pinus strobus*) and eastern white cedar (*Thuja occidentalis*). Today, they continue to be clipped in formal tiered geometry. Topiary makes for an exuberant multi-generational horticultural extravaganza. American holly (*Ilex opaca*) is another native that can be clipped into formal geometric hedges or abstractly pruned into enigmatic ovoid shapes.

RIGHT Topiary withstanding winter well at Longwood Gardens

BELOW Topiaries at the H. H. Hunnewell Arboretum

When trying your hand at topiary, keep in mind that symmetrical repetition may give a sense of rest while also focusing the eye. The deliberate close placement of two repeated forms in the garden concentrates your vision and creates a focal point.

CLOUD PRUNING

Asian gardeners have long drawn inspiration from plants' intrinsic properties and then methodically used this vision to shape trees and shrubs into abstract forms to expose their true qualities. The stylized art of cloud pruning often mimics configurations derived from a tree's exposure to the natural elements found at the seashore and mountaintop. Cloud pruning distills a tree's essence by singling out structural branches and celebrating them, clipping them into oblique shapes. The beauty of this unique, abstract sculptural ensemble transcends any societal associations and stands on the tenets universal to all art.

Cloud pruning lays out a distinct modulation of curved surfaces. The transient patterns of light, glare, and shadow formed in traceries across the spaced arrangement of hemispherical orbs gives a simulation of movement. This pruning art has transformed static trees into incredible lively sculptures that impart a vitality into the frozen winter garden.

Sometimes the seemingly incongruous qualities of absurdity, amusement, and beauty merge together. Unexpectedly coming upon a line of trees in a strip-mall parking lot median that are pruned, topiary fashion, into globes seemed at first glance to be the height of silliness.

In this notable private garden in Rhode Island, *Ilex opaca*, *Cedrus atlantica*, and *Pinus parviflora* have been indulgently clipped in a cloud-pruned fashion for more than fifty years.

These *Cornus mas* have been adeptly pruned into a topiary form. From their appearance, this pruning took many years.

The rounded branched ball on top of a standard straight trunk certainly holds attention. Cornelian cherry blooms with yellow flowers in late winter to early spring. The flower buds are set in late summer on ripened growth and would be ruined by indiscriminately timed shearing. This anonymous horticultural artist has obviously heeded Cornelian cherry's chronology of flower-bud development. The regimented topiary balls, blooming with lemon yellow flowers and dusted with a confection of white snow, attain the status of beauty through their charm. They are, in fact, an inspiration.

PLEACHING

Pleaching is a method of training and pruning trees into narrow, rectilinear panels of hedges or enclosing bowers. Pleaching methods are generally applied to deciduous trees. Their winter aspect is much more complex than a simple flat veneer of green foliage. The wintertime leafless framework of a pleached hedge of fastigiate beech (*Fagus sylvatica* 'Dawyckii') is a wiry filigree of gray-barked, vertical branches and intertwined twigs. This multitude of exposed branches magnifies the pleached hedge's dimensional presence in the winter garden.

Upright-growing forms of European hornbeam (*Carpinus betulus* 'Fastigiata') as well as European beech lend themselves to being pleached and pruned into narrow walls. Both of these trees form adventitious buds that are hidden along mature stems and branches.

Trees that bloom with spring flowers, such as magnolia and crabapple, make excellent candidates for pleaching. Star magnolia (*Magnolia stellata*) lends itself to architectural pruning. Its beautiful light gray bark is revealed in a winter garden. A timely pruning schedule must be heeded to preserve the fuzzy winter flower buds and their successive white spring flowers.

Flowering crabapples (*Malus* spp.) are malleable to many pruning techniques, pleaching to pruning as an espalier. Dwarf forms such as 'Cinderella' and 'Tina' are top grafted onto the straight bole of an understock.

Dawn redwood (*Metasequoia glyptostroboides*) is a deciduous conifer that grows to be a striking specimen. Its tapered trunk and ascending branches are sheathed in orange-tinged bark. This ancient tree also responds positively to present-day pleaching.

Many academic volumes have been written and published by landscape historians and garden scholars about Dumbarton Oaks in Washington, D.C. They recount the story of the Bliss family, their collaboration with landscape designer Beatrix Farrand, her superlative landscape vision, and its amazing mockup and execution. Also written and recorded are the subsequent modifications made to the garden upon Dumbarton Oaks's entry to a new life in the realm of public gardens and as an associate of Harvard

Fagus sylvatica 'Purpurea' awaiting pruning, at bud break from pleaching, and one year after pleaching

The beauty of pleached beech in the winter landscape is its coppery marcescent foliage.

Magnolia stellata may be pleached into a low hedge.

University. Even with this precognition, my visit to Dumbarton Oaks for the first time is forever etched in my mind. In early spring of 1985, I made arrangements to experience, explore, and photograph Farrand's masterpiece. I have since made several pilgrimages to Dumbarton Oaks.

The garden's own *presence* is almost too indescribable for words. For me, of all of the garden's aesthetic and horticultural climaxes, the hornbeam ellipse stands out. The ellipse is a level garden space set within a steep hillside. It is circumscribed with a spaced double row of American hornbeam (*Carpinus caroliniana*), pleached and clipped into an aerial hedge. The simple form of this floating, horizontal hedge holds an incredible energetic force, that of dynamic harmony. The regular uniform lines of its

I have trained a pleached hedge of *Malus* 'Cinderella' into a double row of horizontal cordons.

clipped, curved rectilinear shape offer symmetrical repetition, an echo of the site's even contour, and at the same instance also emphasize a stark contrast to the hillside that looms upward and falls below. Held above a series of spaced, muscular gray hornbeam trunks, this floating, horizontal pleached hedge moves the eye to focus on its elevated level plane. The perched band of clipped branches can be construed as a ring beam, which implies support to an enormous transparent dome. The makeup of this garden and its interplay with space and volume is as complex as it is simple. The emotions I perceived in the garden,

transfixed on the mesmerizing pleached hornbeams, was similar to that of being in a great domed cathedral: exhilaration and reverence. Not such a bad accomplishment for a bunch of clipped *Carpinus*.

The stature and branching habit of Japanese maples constitute sculptural qualities that are also very suitable for pleaching. I planted a linear arrangement of four 'Osakazuki' Japanese maples (*Acer palmatum* 'Osakazuki') as a structural component framing an entry garden. Their branches are pleached, though loosely, into a uniform horizontal panel above a hedge of 'Compacta' inkberry holly (*Ilex glabra* 'Compacta').

The solitary form of Serbian spruce (*Picea omorika*) is a vertical counterpoint in the foreground. 'Osaka-zuki' sports exceptional red foliage in fall and forms a branched framework for icy coatings in the winter.

Pleached bowers provide a rare bit of garden enchantment. In 1998, I planted a circular bower of crab-apples that separates a new garden from the elliptical swimming pool and open space beyond. It leads into a mixed herbaceous garden. When in bloom, the bower is a fragrant white cloud that casts a pattern of cool shade in contrast to the sunny borders. The garden was planted in August 1998, and six *Malus* ×'Sutyzam', or Sugar Tyme crabapple, form the bower. Sugar Tyme is a highly disease-resistant selection and blooms with fragrant flowers in May, followed by a myriad of small red fruit. These are very persistent, lasting through winter and even into the following spring.

These crabapples were planted around the circumference of an eighteen-foot-diameter circle. The curved perimeter is marked into eight portions, with positions one and five left open to provide a space to walk through. After several years of development, training wires were strung across the circular bower to make a frame to tie down and bend the longest

A bower of *Malus* Sugar Tyme, a showstopping focal point year-round

growth of branches and establish a closed canopy. After several more years of shaping and training, the bower was structurally complete. It is now pruned once a year, in late August or early September.

ESPALIER

To espalier is to radically prune and train a tree into a two-dimensional configuration. It necessitates thinning and narrowing down the branch structure of a tree or shrub to form a flat plane. An espalier may be attached to a wall or other support system. Fruit trees are often grown into espalier in order to make thrifty use of space. The ornamental qualities of an espaliered tree are not as stripped down as the form implies: to the contrary, an espalier has great impact. Its form gives structural contrast to garden surfaces, as well as a decorative tracery of branches to blank walls. It also provides a garden design opportunity in spaces too small to grow a tree to its conventional size. The configuration of espaliered branches can range from informal to formal. They can be arranged as an abstract representation of a tree's natural, scaffolded

After autumn's leaf drop, the bower is transformed to a canopy of shiny red fruit. Its form and colorful fruit carry on through snow and ice.

Pruning a pear espalier (*Pyrus*) at the Allen C. Haskell Public Gardens in New Bedford, Massachusetts

Fagus sylvatica 'Purpurea Pendula' espalier on a private residence

form, or geometrically ordered in right angles and spaced in a uniform regiment of horizontal cordons.

One specific espalier of a weeping purple beech (*Fagus sylvatica* 'Purpurea Pendula') is certainly an exemplar of all of the ornamental virtues this abstract form of pruning imparts. This innovative espalier is the artistic creation of horticulturist and landscape designer Gary Koller and resides in a private Boston garden. The purple weeping beech is trained onto a tall, gabled wall and faces a freestanding green weeping beech on the other side of a driveway. The espaliered beech is planted in a narrow bed between the house foundation and pavement, in accompaniment with the variegated winter foliage of kuma bamboo (*Sasa veitchii*). The curtain of pendulous branches adds depth and texture to the shingle facade. The weeping beech is attached to the house with stainless steel eye bolts and plastic-coated ties.

Another remarkable espalier exists at Chanticleer in Wayne, Pennsylvania. This example was grown from a fine-textured rosemary willow (*Salix elaeagnos*), and its espaliered silhouette appears like a feather lightly stroking a three-story stucco wall. Holding true to Chanticleer's avant-garde, changeable garden display, this particular rosemary willow espalier previously exhibited three vertically ascending cordons!

Another favorite tree for this purpose is southern magnolia (*Magnolia grandiflora*), espaliered on the brick facade of Dumbarton Oaks by Beatrix Farrand. Finally, and with special regard to its place in the winter garden, witch hazel can also be trained into a single-trunked tree form. To achieve this affect, it is often grafted high on a standard understock of *Hamamelis virginiana* or *Parrotia persica*. Various cultivars of witch hazel can be used to make an attractive winter-blooming espalier.

Regardless of technique, consider playing up the structure of the winter landscape with ornamental pruning practices. Highlight patterns and forms that add focus to the garden and even show off through drifts of snow. Most of all, have fun clipping, pleaching, and espaliering.

LEFT AND BELOW An espalier of *Salix elaeagnos* at Chanticleer

An espalier of *Tilia cordata*

Magnolia grandiflora modestly espaliered at Dumbarton Oaks (left) and in a private garden in Hopkinton, Rhode Island (right). The latter is attached to a freestanding frame that echoes the outline of the house facade in a veneer of glossy green leaves.

PART IV
SEASONAL CARE AND MAINTENANCE

Chapter Fourteen

Planting Permanent Pots

I have been exploring the wild landscapes of Maine since my youth, and I have always been intrigued by the outcrops of rock ledges that mysteriously rise up through the surface of the ground. My curiosity has been piqued not just by their geology, but also by the assemblage of plants that grow in shallow pockets of soil and out of fissured cracks. Conifers that establish a foothold in a favorable niche in these rock outcrops are dwarfed by the harsh and restrictive environment. Their contorted forms mimic the meticulously pruned and trained trees that are cultivated in the ancient Japanese art of bonsai. These granite ledges form a magical, lilliputian garden.

The ability of arborvitae, spruce, juniper, and pine to grow in such a hostile environment is remarkable. Their roots spread near the soil surface and are also prized in cracks in the rock. There is not even a degree difference between the frigid winter air temperature and the ground. There is no temperature buffer for the roots that deep loam soils and mulches in other locales provide. The ability of these plants to survive in this unique, bleak habitat validates anecdotal evidence of the hardiness of their roots. This experience of seeing these cold-hardy plants along the rocky coast of Maine promoted my passion for growing plants in permanently planted outdoor containers. They can also add life and enviable dimension to the winter garden.

Most everyone has had an indoor potted plant or two, perhaps an assortment of African violets thriving by an east-facing window over the kitchen sink, or a collection of cacti and succulents basking in hot southern exposure. Growing tender or tropical plants outside in containers is also a routine practice for gardeners, and numerous books have been written about this practice.

PLANT SELECTION

There is little literature on the subject of winter-hardy containers. For more than forty years, I have grown trees, shrubs, and perennials successfully in permanent containers year-round outdoors. The first time I used a permanent planter in a client's landscape was in 1982. A topiary form of yew (*Taxus cuspidata* 'Capitata') was planted into a thirty-six-inch diameter stoneware rolled-rim pot. It has been a winter feature and a focal point in an entrance garden ever since. In our home garden, *Thuja occidentalis* 'Rheingold', a favorite dwarf conifer with chartreuse foliage, graces a complementary cobalt-blue pot. When potted, a dwarf Chinese elm (*Ulmus parvifolia* 'Seiju') has the sculptural bearing of a bonsai, without the painstaking effort of training.

In November 2002, I taught a workshop at the Scott Arboretum in Swarthmore, Pennsylvania on planting and growing winter-hardy, permanent containers. Over the last twenty years, it has been gratifying to see so many permanently planted containers added to their gardens. The superbly landscaped grounds of the Swarthmore College campus and the horticultural collections of the Scott Arboretum are exemplary. The

A witch hazel in a container at the Scott Arboretum of Swarthmore College in Pennsylvania

result of this artistic integration adds a tremendous, broad depth to the arboretum and its educational and aesthetic experiences. It is an environment that is rarely found in other arboreta.

When planting permanent pots, the first matter to consider is the selection of plants. Many species of conifers in the following genera are rated to be cold hardy in Zones 2 through 4: *Abies*, *Juniperus*, *Picea*, *Pinus*, and *Thuja*. These are plants that can withstand winter temperatures of minus twenty to minus fifty degrees Fahrenheit. It is best to select plants for permanent pots that are at least two hardiness zones colder than the regional hardiness zone.

Some plants, though perfectly hardy when planted in the ground, have roots that are not as immune to cold when raised in container nursery production. Hollies are one of many plants known to have cold-sensitive roots. Severe winter temperatures can cause damage and death to hollies grown in pots, even when protected in a covered hoop house.

POT MATERIALS

Weatherproof pots are made from many different materials. Some options are rot-resistant wood, cast stone, lead, and zinc. Durable plastics and fiberglass are lightweight and can mimic heavy terracotta clay containers. I am particularly fond of durable stoneware pots made with strong clay and a heavy mix of grog. Stoneware, even unglazed, becomes vitreous from its high firing and does not absorb water like soft, low-fired earthenware pots.

To prevent the breakage of stoneware containers, it is essential that pots are filled with potting soil

I have grown dwarf *Pinus virginiana* 'Wate's Golden' (left), Thuja occidentalis 'DeGroot's Spire' (right), and many other conifers in permanent pots over the years.

Vaccinium macrocarpon is cold hardy to Zone 2; these cranberries are in a suspended trough container made from a length of large four-inch angle iron.

throughout the winter. If they are empty, they will fill with water and freeze. Freezing and expanding ice will even break granite! Also raise the container off the ground by setting it on several bricks to ensure drainage. This will prevent stress fractures that occur when the bottom of the pot freezes to the ground but the top is warmed by the winter sun.

Making square planter boxes from wood is not a new concept. In late seventeenth-century France, at the Château de Versailles, tree boxes were developed to display and grow orange trees in the garden's elaborate parterres. Since the citrus trees were not cold-hardy, they were moved into a glass-glazed orangerie for the winter. The boxes were made with cast-iron frames and removable wooden sides. Contemporary versions of this classic, Versailles-style planter still add an architectural geometry to the garden.

Tufa is a natural, porous limestone rock prized by alpine plant enthusiasts and rock gardeners. Hypertufa is a fabricated amalgamation of Portland cement, peat moss, and perlite. It can be cast or modeled into both geometric and naturalistic, stone-like troughs. I use a hypertufa recipe of equal proportions by volume of those three ingredients. Concrete dyes can be added to customize the color. The strength and durability of a hypertufa trough are achieved through the process of curing; that is, covering and sealing the newly formed container with plastic for a minimum of ten days—this allows for a long, damp cure. Ideally, the finished hypertufa container should be placed in the shade of trees to age; this will hasten the development of patina.

Choose containers with shapes and colors that add a sculptural quality to the garden. The size of the container should also be large enough to prevent frequent drying. I recommend pots that are twenty-four inches in diameter or larger for small trees and shrubs.

POTTING UP

Once plants and containers have been selected, it is time for the potting mix. Drainage and structural stability are the most important factors in making a potting mix. A permanent growing medium will be much different from the soilless peat moss and bark-based mix that is the standard used for seasonal tender plants, sold as "potting mix." That organic soil will substantially break down and decompose in one growing season; it will also shrink and lose its structure.

Permanent pots require a coarse-textured growing mixture composed of one-third loam soil by volume. Add another one-third portion of an equal mixture of aggregates. Combine granules of calcined clay (Turface) with one-half inch of crushed stone or expanded shale. A mixture of compost and peat moss rounds out the organic final third of the soil mix.

WATERING AND FERTILIZING

As with any container-grown plant, watering is essential and should continue through fall. Unlike bonsai trees, permanently potted hardy trees and shrubs do not need a regime of root pruning and repotting. Even after thirty-four years, my dwarf Alberta spruce is thriving with little attention other than watering. The plants will reach and maintain an equilibrium of top growth and root growth. Hardy trees and shrubs should be fertilized infrequently, and only with a slow-release fertilizer.

PLACEMENT

Growing a plant in a container also promotes its presence in the garden, as if raising it on a stage. I have literally elevated a hypertufa trough, displaying it on three-foot-high pipe stilts, and planted it with one of my favorite dwarf conifers, 'Schoodic' jack pine. The added height from the legs allows the container to stand out, an accent against a mixed herbaceous border. In winter, its elevated stance sets it well above drifts of snow.

GREEN ROOFS AND WALLS

While roofs and walls are not pots per se, they are self-contained growing areas with artificial perimeters, so their planting requirements are similar to permanent plantings in pots. Planting a green roof with succulents and sedums (*Sedum* spp.) is no longer extremely rare—green roofs are an important measure to conserve energy and mitigate stormwater discharge. In dense, urban areas, there is often little room for growing trees. Acres of green-planted roof surfaces help reduce the intensity of urban heat islands in summer.

Taking a cue from the plants that flourish on flat roofs, I put a slant on the proposition. I designed and constructed an outdoor shower space that is

Dwarf *Pinus banksiana* 'Schoodic' planted in a stoneware urn adorns an entrance landing. Its evergreen branches extend over the rim of the container and emphasize its cascading form, making it much more noticeable and prominent than if it were planted at ground level.

I planted *Pinus rigida* 'Sand Beach' in a shallow hypertufa tray placed atop stout legs of tree trunks. *Sibbaldiopsis tridentata* covers the soil surface in a planting theme that mimics its natural habitat on the coast of Maine.

enclosed with louvered walls planted with sedums. The containers that hold the plants are stainless-steel trays that measure twenty inches by forty-eight inches, with a two-inch high lip. A spaced series of these trays are attached to wooden posts and positioned at a forty-five-degree angle. The planted walls are not irrigated; the planting medium is lightweight, with aggregates of pumice and Turface. The sedums' foliage remains attractive year-round. Even in winter, this planting is colored in shades of green and reddish bronze. Plants are just amazing.

My first professional horticultural employment after graduating from the University of Maine in 1976 was to work with Ludwig Hoffman at his nursery in

The sedum shower in July

Bloomfield, Connecticut. The urban and suburban landscapes were a foreign environment from the nature that I knew from growing up in Maine.

One of Lud's corporate clients was the Constitution Plaza in Hartford, Connecticut. This landmark of urban renewal was designed by architect Charles DuBose and landscape architects associated with Sasaki, Dawson and DeMay in 1964. It is a roof garden, elevated above the street level, that covers a below-ground parking garage. Constitution Plaza encompasses more than three acres of terraces and planted landscape around commercial buildings. Gumdrop-shaped, pleached littleleaf linden (*Tilia cordata* 'Greenspire') is planted in large, six-foot-diameter concrete planters. These are accompanied by honeylocust (*Gleditsia triacanthus* 'Shademaster') and star magnolia (*Magnolia stellata*). Ovoid-shaped, turf-covered mounds planted with weeping willow (*Salix ×elegantissima*) are actually large planters retained by an eighteen-inch-high concrete curb. The perimeter of the plaza forms a linear concrete trough, and it is planted with a hedge of dark green yew (*Taxus ×media* 'Densiformis').

In retrospect, there is a parity between the dissimilar landscapes of the Maine coast and downtown Hartford. The massive expanses of exposed bedrock and granite ledges of Maine provide similar growing conditions to the monumental, reinforced-concrete slab that supports Constitution Plaza. The ornamental beauty and life-giving spirit of plants unify these microcosms. However large or small, adorn your winter garden with hardy plants in containers. It is a prime opportunity to add the beauty of plants to spaces that have no soil to cultivate.

Chapter Fifteen

Protecting Plants

Successfully growing hardy plants in gardens throughout northern temperate regions requires a keen knowledge of their cultural and environmental requirements. Though these may vary wildly, familiarity with a plant's cold tolerance is a singular priority. Hardy plants are referenced in categories that correspond to the standards of USDA hardiness zones. Regional zone maps define geographic areas by their annual average minimum temperature. An accurate interpretation of hardiness zone designations is necessary in order to select the best plants for your garden.

Hardiness is more complex than simply assigning a standard zone number to plants. The reality of growing hardy plants that survive cold winters involves nuance. Flower buds, for instance, are much more susceptible to cold damage than leaf buds. Many trees and shrubs of the same species grow across an extensive native habitat—one species might range from Maine to Florida. The hardiness of a particular plant selection is related to its regional genotype, and this may differ from plants selected from other members of the same species. Genetic differences in plants may occur due to being separated by vast geographic distances and over eons in time. This can translate into variations in cold tolerance.

The degree of winter cold is not uniform within a region. It varies considerably within broad topographical areas, as well as small spaces inside the bounds of a garden. The dates of a hard frost, for instance, can vary greatly, even within a few miles of separation. A hilltop location may not get a freeze, whereas low-lying land along a stream basin may be white with frost on the same day. The density of cold air causes it to settle, which can make valleys colder than higher elevations. Winter temperatures along coastal areas are moderated in a gradient by the relative warmth of water versus land.

What's more, in Massachusetts, the period toward the end of the growing season when hardy woody plants prepare for winter runs from late September through early October, when these plants actively move sugars from leaves to the storage tissues of stems and roots. This metabolic process is called hardening off, and it is critical for their winter survival. Sufficient autumn rainfall for good soil moisture is an important factor in this process, and extreme dry soil conditions can be detrimental, resulting in dieback of the terminal twigs and flower buds the following spring.

Erratic precipitation patterns are the reality of global warming and climate change. If there is a severe lack of natural rainfall, supplemental watering will be needed. Deep watering of recently installed plants and even established ones may be necessary.

To a gardener, the impact of these and other subtle climatic differences is worth exploring. Identification of niches in growing conditions within the garden provides insight into the refined details of winter garden environs.

MULCHES

A layer of organic mulch in the garden is an important year-round horticultural practice. Mulches are layers of chopped leaves, shredded bark, or wood chips added on top of the soil around the crowns of plants. During the growing season, mulch layers suppress weeds and protect roots from extreme heat. Most importantly, they help retain soil moisture. Adding a mulch layer to the garden can help alleviate the effects of drought. As they break down, organic mulches also add to the soil's structure.

Snow cover is nature's natural winter mulch, yet it is certainly not reliable. In fall, the addition of an extra layer of organic mulch helps keep the ground cold and prevents a cycle of thawing and freezing on the open ground throughout the winter. This pattern can cause the soil to heave, dislodging plants. Winter

mulch can also be as beautiful as it is functional: A layer of pine needles presents a well-groomed winter garden.

Utilizing fallen autumn leaves as a winter mulch is both economically and environmentally prudent. I designed a garden for a small city plot where a large oak tree shades the garden and stone patio. A substantial quantity of leaves fall from the oak every autumn. They are not removed and hauled away but instead raked up and shredded in place. The chopped leaves are then spread in the garden around shrubs and perennials. A final topping of amber-colored white pine (*Pinus strobus*) needles gives the garden an elegantly refined look for the winter. The layer of pine needles and leaf mulch actually lasts through the following growing season.

Pine straw is a uniquely southern horticultural commodity. It is found in garden supply stores from Virginia south to Georgia and Florida. The fallen needles of longleaf pine (*Pinus palustris*), slash pine (*Pinus elliottii*), and loblolly pine (*Pinus taeda*) are boxed or baled for use as garden mulch. Longleaf pine needles measure eight to sixteen inches in length. Loblolly needles are shorter, only four to six inches long.

There is no cottage industry in New England that gathers and markets the needles of our native white pine as a mulch. However, white pine trees are plentiful, and though the length of their needles is a meager four inches, they can be a free source of beautiful garden mulch.

In November, I rake up and bag the freshly fallen needles. Pine needles form a loose mulch layer that doesn't compact or hold excessive moisture around plant stems and crowns. It is an ideal mulch for Mediterranean plants that resent wet winter soils, such as

White pine needles used as a mulch that also defines a path

lavender and cyclamen. The acidity of the pine needles retards their decomposition, so they last as mulch, but they do not appreciably lower the pH of the soils.

GUARDING AGAINST SUN DAMAGE

Mulches can mitigate winter's extreme temperatures on the crowns of herbaceous perennials and the roots of trees and shrubs, but the low angle of the winter sun is another element that deserves the gardener's

Pine needles make an ideal mulch for Mediterranean plants, including cyclamen.

attention. By mid-February, the intensity of sunlight has increased significantly from the dim days of the winter solstice. Wintertime bark damage from sun, known as southwest injury, is fittingly named for the compass-bearing relationship of the sun to the trunk of a tree. The combination of the sun's oblique angle and its afternoon position in the southwest sky focuses its energy on the vertical angle of the surface of tree trunks. Young trees, and those with thin, pale-colored bark, are the most susceptible to this damage. Sun-scald and bark-split injuries can easily be prevented by wrapping the trunks with a temporary winter sheath of cloth or paper.

A southwest orientation should also be avoided when choosing a garden position for tender plants. This is especially necessary for those that are on the upper edge of the winter hardiness zone. An easterly placement is more benign; the north-facing wall of a building is also a protected location, as it is always out of the direct rays of the winter sun.

PROTECTING AGAINST HEAVY SNOW AND TEMPERATURE EXTREMES

The leaves of hardy evergreens have evolved to withstand harsh winter weather. Some developed their survival with an association with deep drifts of protective snow cover. I grow heaths and heathers in mild areas of Cape Cod, Massachusetts, without any extra winter protection. However, in other parts of New England, these sub-shrubs benefit from some extra protection from the desiccating effects of the winter sun and wind. A light covering of cut branches of evergreen boughs such as spruce and fir is a traditional method to afford them winter protection.

Garland Farm in Bar Harbor, Maine was the last home and garden of landscape architect Beatrix Farrand. The garden is filled with choice specimens she transplanted there in 1955 from her former Reef Point Gardens. *Stewartia koreana*, *Enkianthus campanulatus*, and *Metasequoia glyptostroboides* are cherished plants from her close friendship with Charles Sargent and the Arnold Arboretum. The Beatrix Farrand Society, dedicated to preserving her horticultural legacy, now stewards the property and maintains the gardens. Garland Farm is listed on the National Register of Historic Places.

The terrace garden here is predominantly planted with lavender, heath, and heather, where the gardeners currently employ an innovative form of winter protection for Farrand's beloved collection of the latter pair. The traditional use of cut spruce boughs caused a detrimental amount of moisture to be held against their foliage. Boughs also shielded snow from accumulating around the plants, which typically provides insulation from winter cold. Their new solution is a variation of the old-fashioned slatted snow fence. They used a scrim made of green-colored plastic, a type of construction barrier mesh. This cover is secured with stakes, catches drifting snow, and also shades the heaths and heathers from the winter sun. This protective structure is an unobtrusive green camouflage in the garden.

Tailor-made burlap cocoons are one method to provide protection from winter desiccation. These create prominently bagged trees that present an odd winter prospect. Though burlap shrouds may be effective in mitigating winter damage, at best, they should be used discreetly in the garden—they're as appropriate as displaying laundry hung on a clothesline in the front yard. A much better solution, which is also aesthetically pleasing, would be to sensitively evaluate the garden site and design; then select an appropriate tough and hardy plant to grow, rather than wrapping conifers in a mummy-like manner.

Winter snow is not always the light, fluffy, harmless kind that blankets trees in a lovely cottony cover. Heavy, wet snow and ice wreak havoc with plants as well as utility lines. Some upright-growing evergreens are particularly prone to damage because their foliage holds the heavy, wet snow and causes the vertical stems to splay open. The vertical stems of fastigiate

yews and 'Graham Blandy' boxwood, for example, can be ruinously damaged. In the fall, prepare these fastigiate evergreens for winter with a simple cinch of sisal rope. The sisal rope will degrade within the year and will not pose a girdling risk to trunks, even if it is not promptly removed.

Garland Farm's terrace garden, planted with heath and heathers, receives snow fence and some sun protection from an inexpensive plastic scrim.

Burlap cocoons are effective but always unsightly.

Several A-frames are grouped together to support the spreading branches of a weeping Japanese maple from the weight of excess ice and snow.

A different form of winter barrier is this maypole-like steel frame. It protects this *Sciadopitys verticillata* from ice breakage.

Fastigiate deciduous trees are also at risk from heavy snow and ice damage. Protect elegant pleached hedges of beech against winter weather by stringing a pair of binding lines the length of the hedge and just above where the lowest major branches join the canopy.

Temporary structures made of sturdy wood or steel can be placed in the garden to protect plants over the winter season. Wooden A-frame braces resembling sandwich boards are a strong defense that protects plants from ice damage.

DEFYING DEER

The scourge of white-tailed deer browsing and destroying valuable plants requires dedicated and sometimes expensive countermeasures. Since the 1980s, I have experienced significant environmental and climatic-disruptive changes that have impacted ornamental horticulture. The extent of the significance of the deer problem becomes clear when all the standardized, commercial plant labels suddenly include the term "deer-proof" whenever they can plausibly claim it.

The incidence of Lyme disease, first recognized in 1975 in Lyme, Connecticut, is one of the fastest-growing vector-borne infections in the United States. It is correlated with the expanded population growth of white-tailed deer. As with many ecological systems, there are many interconnected factors that make solutions complex and difficult, though as far as gardeners are concerned the answer is simple: Deer and gardens don't mix.

The installation of an eight-foot-high deer fence around a garden is one concrete solution. Shirley and Peter Williams are dedicated and passionate gardeners who run Brigham Hill Farm in North Grafton, Massachusetts. When the match between the deer and their garden became a rivalry, the garden won decisively. A large section of the property was totally enclosed with an eight-foot-high fence made of six-inch square wire mesh. We designed and commissioned a black powder-coated steel fence to enclose the front of the property. The welded steel fence is made up of three-eighths-inch square spindles spaced six inches apart. It is installed suspended above an existing field-stone wall that runs along the road for the length of the property. The combined height of the stone wall and the fence creates a handsome, deer-proof barrier. The fence's design is unusual in that it has no top rail. The presentation of uninterrupted, rhythmically spaced vertical lines makes the fence appear more transparent. Though it is a substantial barrier, it doesn't detract from the view of the eighteenth-century farmhouse from the road.

Various deer repellents are more effective than others. Some, like thiram, are sprayed on foliage directly. It slightly discolors the foliage of evergreens, though

Various approaches to deer netting

deer browsing would be a worse blemish. Repeated applications may be necessary.

Seasonally established barriers work best if the intrusion of deer into the garden is only in winter. In late November, I attach a six-foot-high, heavy plastic mesh to stakes that surround the yews and arborvitae in my garden.

The impact of weather on the winter garden has its challenges. Whether it is feast or famine, with a little forethought, the beauty of the winter garden will easily prevail, providing enjoyment for many, many years to come.

Acknowledgments

I would like to recognize and thank the many friends and landscape clients whose beautiful gardens I have photographed: Bertha Atwater, Allen and Sarah Berry, Emily Harrison and James Boyd, Bill Cannon, Joan and Michael Even, Andrew Freedman and Dr. Paula Bellin, Linda and Kevan Gibson, John Gwynn and Mikel Folcarelli, David Hagan, Judith and Dr. Larry Karlin, Gary Koller, Philip and Jane Kratsch, Dr. Ellen Lathi, Barbara Legg, Suzanne Mahler, Dr. Arthur McAuley, Ellen and Duncan McFarland, Louis Raymond, Jonathan and Eugenie Shaw, Susan and Raymond Shaw, Rebecca Sholes and Carlos Porras, Louise and Larry Shwartz, Holly Smith, Joanne Stuart, Laurie Tarnell, Maureen Taylor and Dexter Strong, Kathy and Chris Tracy, Bill Varnell and Mary Knasas, and Shirley and Peter Williams.

I must also acknowledge the many botanic gardens and arboreta whose plant collections contain vast horticultural wealth. I explored this treasure trove to compile the photographs that richly enhance this book.

I am indebted to the Arnold Arboretum of Harvard University; the H. H. Hunnewell Estate and Arboretum; New England Botanic Garden at Tower Hill; the Massachusetts Horticultural Society; Bedrock Gardens; Blithewold Mansion, Gardens, and Arboretum; the Polly Hill Arboretum; Allen C. Haskell Public Gardens; the Morris Arboretum and Gardens of the University of Pennsylvania; the Scott Arboretum of Swarthmore College; the United States National Arboretum; the New York Botanical Garden; Wave Hill; Naumkeag; the Met Cloisters; Snug Harbor Cultural Center and Botanic Garden; Mt. Cuba Center; Chanticleer; Longwood Gardens; Dumbarton Oaks; the Isabella Stewart Gardner Museum; Fallingwater; Mount Auburn Cemetery; Swan Point Cemetery; Abby Aldrich Rockefeller Garden; Asticou Azalea Garden; Thuya Garden; Garland Farm; Coastal Maine Botanical Gardens; Buzzards Bay Brewing; Pleasant Run Nursery; Summer Hill Nursery; and Sylvan Nursery.

Photo Credits

All photos are by the author with the exception of the following:

Pat Breen, Oregon State University; page 68 (bottom)
John Roger Palmour, page 8

ALAMY

Botany Vision, page 53
Botanic World, page 60 (bottom, right)
Digital-Fotofusion Gallery, page 37 (right)
Tim Gainey, page 90 (top)
Bob Gibbons, page 88
Colleen Miniuk-Sperry, page 99
Ginn Tinn Photography, page 77 (top, left)
John Martin, page 93 (bottom, right)
Matthew Taylor, page 92 (left)
Thrillerfillerspiller, page 122 (bottom, left)

DREAMSTIME

Annakazantseva; pages 90 (middle, center), 93 (top, left)
Anthony Baggett, page 90 (bottom)
Bonandbon Dw, page 32 (top, left)
Irina Borsuchenko, page 57 (bottom, middle)
Ala Botnarescu, page 143 (top, left)
John Caley, page 57 (bottom, left)
Marianne Campolongo, page 90 (top, left)

Rob Lumen Captum, page 46
Ericaimama, page 69 (top)
Steve Estvanik, page 182 (right)
Julie Feinstein; pages 37 (bottom, left), 42 (top), 144 (bottom), 145 (bottom)
Bob Grabowski, page 142 (center)
Hellmann1, page 89
John Holmes, page 93 (bottom, left)
Tracy Immordino; pages 96 (left), 98 (left)
Jennifergauld, page 102
Jundream, page 182 (left)
Karin59, page 152 (bottom, left)
Yorozu Kitamura; pages 31 (bottom, left), 32 (top, right), 43 (top, right), 57 (top), 152 (left)
Krisata, page 61 (left)
Nikolai Kurzenko; pages 45 (left), 123 (right)
Llmckinne; pages 31 (middle, right), 90 (middle, right)
Loflo69, page 41 (left)
David Maddock, page 98 (right)
Paul Maguire, page 153 (left)
Marinodenisenko; pages 39 (bottom), 60 (bottom, left), 62,
Markzhu, page 183 (bottom)
Kateryna Mashevych, page 44
Heather Mcardle, page 96 (right)
Kim Nelson, page 116 (bottom, right)
Michal Paulus, page 31 (bottom, right)
Simona Pavan; pages 47 (bottom), 122 (top, left), 142 (bottom), 156

Gaid Phitthayakormsilp, page 123 (bottom)

Stephan Pietzko, page 93 (top, center)

Rbiedermann, page 153 (top, right)

Rvo233, page 55 (middle, right)

Sagegardenherbs, page 57 (bottom, right)

Tetiana Soares, page 31 (top, left)

Steve5181, page 31 (top, right)

StrippedPixel, page 183 (top)

Hiroshi Tanaka, page 122 (middle, left)

Gerald D. Tang, page 151 (center, right)

Edwin Verin, page 184

Iva Villi; pages 37 (top, left), 64 (bottom, right), 95 (center), 120 (top, left)

Christian Weiß, page 92 (center)

Wirestock, pages 100–101

Zanozaru, page 48 (right, middle)

Zniehf, page 125 (bottom)

FLICKR

Bob Mayer, p. 105 (right)

GAP

Thomas Alamy, page 59 (left)

Adrian Bloom; pages 67 (bottom), 79 (Foggy Bottom, The Bressingham Gardens, Norfolk), 94 (Winter Garden, The Bressingham Gardens, Norfolk)

Jonathan Buckley, page 92 (right)

Karen Chapman, page 87

Liz Every, page 191

Jacqui Hurst, page 28 (top)

Nova Photo Graphik, pages 58 (right), 71 (left)

Howard Rice, page 91 (top [The Winter Garden, Cambridge Botanic Gardens] and bottom)

Evgeniya Vlasova, page 48 (left)

Juliette Wade, page 73 (top, left)

Richard Wareham, page 48 (top, right)

Jo Whitworth, page 103

iSTOCK

Billy_Fam, page 39 (top, left)

Hsvrs, page 123 (left)

pixelpot, page 36

Rcerruti, page 157 (left)

SHUTTERSTOCK

Yingna Cai, page 31 (middle, left)

Danita Delimont, page 81

Nahhana, page 39 (top, right)

Olga52, page 93 (top, right)

Mike Russell, page 95 (left)

Index

About the Author

Mark Pagliarini

Born and raised in Maine, **Warren Leach** has a lifelong passion for plants. After his graduation from the University of Maine at Orono, his horticultural career led him to nurseries in Connecticut and Massachusetts. Today, he and his wife Debi Hogan own Tranquil Lake Nursery in Rehoboth, Massachusetts. Warren is an award-winning landscape designer. Images of his garden design at Brigham Hill Farm in North Grafton, Massachusetts are archived at the Smithsonian Institution in Washington, D.C. In 2010, he was awarded a gold medal from the Massachusetts Horticultural Society. Following the example of his many mentors, Warren shares his love of gardens and his horticultural expertise through writing, public speaking, and teaching. He has taught courses at the Arnold Arboretum of Harvard University, the Scott Arboretum at Swarthmore College, the Massachusetts Horticultural Society, Brown University, the Rhode Island School of Design, the New England Botanic Garden at Tower Hill, and the Native Plant Trust. His writing has appeared in *Fine Gardening*, *American Nurseryman*, and *Boston* magazines.